THE INSTANT
OF MY DEATH

DEMEURE

MERIDIAN

Crossing Aesthetics

Werner Hamacher

& David E. Wellbery

Editors

Translated by
Elizabeth Rottenberg

Stanford
University
Press

Stanford
California
2000

THE INSTANT
OF MY DEATH

Maurice Blanchot

DEMEURE
FICTION AND TESTIMONY

Jacques Derrida

Support for the translation was provided
by the French Ministry of Culture

Originally published in French as:

for *The Instant of My Death*,
in 1994, Maurice Blanchot, *L'instant de ma mort*,
by Fata Morgana
© Fata Morgana 1994.
Reproduced by permission of Fata Morgana.

for *Demeure: Fiction and Testimony*,
in 1998, Jacques Derrida, *Demeure: Maurice Blanchot*,
by Editions Galilée
© 1998, Editions Galilée.

Printed in the United States of America

CIP data appear at the end of the book

Contents

THE INSTANT
OF MY DEATH

Maurice Blanchot

§ L'instant de ma mort

JE ME SOUVIENS d'un jeune homme—un homme encore jeune—empêché de mourir par la mort même—et peut-être l'erreur de l'injustice.

Les Alliés avaient réussi à prendre pied sur le sol français. Les Allemands, déjà vaincus, luttaient en vain avec une inutile férocité.

Dans une grande maison (le Château, disait-on), on frappa à la porte plutôt timidement. Je sais que le jeune homme vint ouvrir à des hôtes qui sans doute demandaient secours.

Cette fois, hurlement: "Tous dehors."

Un lieutenant nazi, dans un français honteusement normal, fit sortir d'abord les personnes les plus âgées, puis deux jeunes femmes.

"Dehors, dehors." Cette fois, il hurlait. Le jeune homme ne cherchait pourtant pas à fuir, mais avançait lentement, d'une manière presque sacerdotale. Le lieutenant le secoua, lui montra des douilles, des balles, il y avait eu manifestement combat, le sol était un sol guerrier.

Le lieutenant s'étrangla dans un langage bizarre, et met-

§ The Instant of My Death

I REMEMBER a young man—a man still young—prevented from dying by death itself—and perhaps the error of injustice.

The Allies had succeeded in getting a foothold on French soil. The Germans, already vanquished, were struggling in vain with useless ferocity.

In a large house (the Château, it was called), someone knocked at the door rather timidly. I know that the young man came to open the door to guests who were presumably asking for help.

This time, a howl: "Everyone outside."

A Nazi lieutenant, in shamefully normal French, made the oldest people exit first, and then two young women.

"Outside, outside." This time, he was howling. The young man, however, did not try to flee but advanced slowly, in an almost priestly manner. The lieutenant shook him, showed him the casings, bullets; there had obviously been fighting; the soil was a war soil.

The lieutenant choked in a bizarre language. And putting the casings, the bullets, a grenade under the nose of

tant sous le nez de l'homme déjà moins jeune (on vieillit vite) les douilles, les balles, une grenade, cria distincte- ment: "Voilà à quoi vous êtes parvenu."

Le nazi mit en rang ses hommes pour atteindre, selon les règles, la cible humaine. Le jeune homme dit: "Faites au moins rentrer ma famille." Soit: la tante (94 ans), sa mère plus jeune, sa sœur et sa belle-sœur, un long et lent cortège, silencieux, comme si tout était déjà accompli.

Je sais—le sais-je—que celui que visaient déjà les Alle- mands, n'attendant plus que l'ordre final, éprouva alors un sentiment de légèreté extraordinaire, une sorte de béati- tude (rien d'heureux cependant),—allégresse souveraine? La rencontre de la mort et de la mort?

A sa place, je ne chercherai pas à analyser ce sentiment de légèreté. Il était peut-être tout à coup invincible. Mort—immortel. Peut-être l'extase. Plutôt le sentiment de compassion pour l'humanité souffrante, le bonheur de n'être pas immortel ni éternel. Désormais, il fut lié à la mort, par une amitié subreptice.

A cet instant, brusque retour au monde, éclata le bruit considérable d'une proche bataille. Les camarades du maquis voulaient porter secours à celui qu'ils savaient en danger. Le lieutenant s'éloigna pour se rendre compte. Les Allemands restaient en ordre, prêts à demeurer ainsi dans une immobilité qui arrêtait le temps.

Mais voici que l'un d'eux s'approcha et dit d'une voix ferme: "Nous, pas allemands, russes," et, dans une sorte de rire: "armée Vlassov," et il lui fit signe de disparaître.

Je crois qu'il s'éloigna, toujours dans le sentiment de légèreté, au point qu'il se retrouva dans un bois éloigné, nommé "Bois des bruyères," où il demeura abrité par les arbres qu'il connaissait bien. C'est dans le bois épais que tout à coup, et après combien de temps, il retrouva le sens du réel. Partout, des incendies, une suite de feu continu,

the man already less young (one ages quickly), he distinctly shouted: "This is what you have come to."

The Nazi placed his men in a row in order to hit, according to the rules, the human target. The young man said, "At least have my family go inside." So it was: the aunt (ninety-four years old); his mother, younger; his sister and his sister-in-law; a long, slow procession, silent, as if everything had already been done.

I know—do I know it—that the one at whom the Germans were already aiming, awaiting but the final order, experienced then a feeling of extraordinary lightness, a sort of beatitude (nothing happy, however)—sovereign elation? The encounter of death with death?

In his place, I will not try to analyze. He was perhaps suddenly invincible. Dead—immortal. Perhaps ecstasy. Rather the feeling of compassion for suffering humanity, the happiness of not being immortal or eternal. Henceforth, he was bound to death by a surreptitious friendship.

At that instant, an abrupt return to the world, the considerable noise of a nearby battle exploded. Comrades from the maquis wanted to bring help to one they knew to be in danger. The lieutenant moved away to assess the situation. The Germans stayed in order, prepared to remain thus in an immobility that arrested time.

Then one of them approached and said in a firm voice, "We're not Germans, Russians," and, with a sort of laugh, "Vlassov army," and made a sign for him to disappear.

I think he moved away, still with the feeling of lightness, until he found himself in a distant forest, named the "Bois des bruyères," where he remained sheltered by trees he knew well. In the dense forest suddenly, after how much time, he rediscovered a sense of the real. Everywhere fires, a continuous succession of fires; all the farms were burning. A little later, he learned that three young

toutes les fermes brûlaient. Un peu plus tard, il apprit que trois jeunes gens, fils de fermiers, bien étrangers à tout combat, et qui n'avaient pour tort que leur jeunesse, avaient été abattus.

Même les chevaux gonflés, sur la route, dans les champs, attestaient une guerre qui avait duré. En réalité, combien de temps s'était-il écoulé? Quand le lieutenant était revenu et qu'il s'était rendu compte de la disparition du jeune châtelain, pourquoi la colère, la rage, ne l'avaient-elles pas poussé à brûler le Château (immobile et majestueux)? C'est que c'était le Château. Sur la façade était inscrite, comme un souvenir indestructible, la date de 1807. Etait-il assez cultivé pour savoir que c'était l'année fameuse de Iéna, lorsque Napoléon, sur son petit cheval gris, passait sous les fenêtres de Hegel qui reconnut en lui "l'âme du monde," ainsi qu'il l'écrivit à un ami? Mensonge et vérité, car, comme Hegel l'écrivit à un autre ami, les Français pillèrent et saccagèrent sa demeure. Mais Hegel savait distinguer l'empirique et l'essentiel. En cette année 1944, le lieutenant nazi eut pour le Château le respect ou la considération que les fermes ne suscitaient pas. Pourtant on fouilla partout. On prit quelque argent; dans une pièce séparée, "la chambre haute," le lieutenant trouva des papiers et une sorte d'épais manuscrit—qui contenait peut-être des plans de guerre. Enfin il partit. Tout brûlait, sauf le Château. Les Seigneurs avaient été épargnés.

Alors commença sans doute pour le jeune homme le tourment de l'injustice. Plus d'extase; le sentiment qu'il n'était vivant que parce que, même aux yeux des Russes, il appartenait à une classe noble.

C'était cela, la guerre: la vie pour les uns, pour les autres, la cruauté de l'assassinat.

Demeurait cependent, au moment où la fusillade n'était plus qu'en attente, le sentiment de légèreté que je ne sau-

men, sons of farmers—truly strangers to all combat, whose only fault was their youth—had been slaughtered.

Even the bloated horses, on the road, in the fields, attested to a war that had gone on. In reality, how much time had elapsed? When the lieutenant returned and became aware the young chatelaine had disappeared, why did anger, rage, not prompt him to burn down the Château (immobile and majestic)? Because it was the Château. On the facade was inscribed, like an indestructible reminder, the date 1807. Was he cultivated enough to know this was the famous year of Jena, when Napoleon, on his small gray horse, passed under the windows of Hegel, who recognized in him the "spirit of the world," as he wrote to a friend? Lie and truth: for as Hegel wrote to another friend, the French pillaged and ransacked his home. But Hegel knew how to distinguish the empirical and the essential. In that year 1944, the Nazi lieutenant had for the Château a respect or consideration that the farms did not arouse. Everything was searched, however. Some money was taken; in a separate room, "the high chamber," the lieutenant found papers and a sort of thick manuscript—which perhaps contained war plans. Finally he left. Everything was burning, except the Château. The Seigneurs had been spared.

No doubt what then began for the young man was the torment of injustice. No more ecstasy; the feeling that he was only living because, even in the eyes of the Russians, he belonged to a noble class.

This was war: life for some, for others, the cruelty of assassination.

There remained, however, at the moment when the shooting was no longer but to come, the feeling of lightness that I would not know how to translate: freed from life? the infinite opening up? Neither happiness, nor un-

rais traduire: libéré de la vie? l'infini qui s'ouvre? Ni bonheur, ni malheur. Ni l'absence de crainte et peut-être déjà
le pas au-delà. Je sais, j'imagine que ce sentiment in-
analysable changea ce qui lui restait d'existence. Comme si
la mort hors de lui ne pouvait désormais que se heurter à la
mort en lui. "Je suis vivant. Non, tu es mort."

happiness. Nor the absence of fear and perhaps already the step beyond. I know, I imagine that this unanalyzable feeling changed what there remained for him of existence. As if the death outside of him could only henceforth collide with the death in him. "I am alive. No, you are dead."

Plus tard, revenu à Paris, il rencontra Malraux. Celui-ci lui raconta qu'il avait été fait prisonnier (sans être reconnu), qu'il avait réussi à s'échapper, tout en perdant un manuscrit. "Ce n'étaient que des réflexions sur l'art, faciles à reconstituer, tandis qu'un manuscrit ne saurait l'être." Avec Paulhan, il fit faire des recherches qui ne pouvaient que rester vaines.

Qu'importe. Seul demeure le sentiment de légèreté qui est la mort même ou, pour le dire plus précisément, l'instant de ma mort désormais toujours en instance.

Later, having returned to Paris, he met Malraux, who said that he had been taken prisoner (without being recognized) and that he had succeeded in escaping, losing a manuscript in the process. "It was only reflections on art, easy to reconstitute, whereas a manuscript would not be." With Paulhan, he made inquiries which could only remain in vain.

What does it matter. All that remains is the feeling of lightness that is death itself or, to put it more precisely, the instant of my death henceforth always in abeyance.

DEMEURE

Jacques Derrida

The first version of this essay was delivered on July 24, 1995, at a conference at the Catholic University of Louvain, to open an international colloquium organized under the direction of Michel Lisse.

The proceedings of that colloquium (*Passions de la littérature: Avec Jacques Derrida*) were published in 1996 by Editions Galilée with this as the lead essay, entitled "Demeure: Fiction et témoignage."

§ Demeure

Fiction and Testimony

"Fiction and Testimony" was at first a provisional and improvised title, a foray of sorts, a way of seeing. I must answer for it today, given that, rightly or wrongly, I prefer to keep it more or less intact.[1] It can be heard now as a minor and displaced echo, indeed, a modest translation, anachronistic and awkward but deliberately distorted: *Dichtung und Wahrheit.* One can also imagine a twisted translation, *voilée*, as one says in French of a wheel after an accident, that its spokes have *buckled*: *Dichtung und Wahrheit* after the fall.

Dichtung is often mistakenly translated as "fiction." I myself have yielded to this bad habit at least once, more than ten years ago, in a context not unrelated to a certain history of Belgium—to which I will return in another way today—the context of the relations between fiction and autobiographical truth. Which is also to say, between literature and death. Speaking then, shortly after his death, of my friend Paul de Man, whose memory I salute since we are here in his country, I wrote the following, which you will perhaps forgive me more easily for citing if I promise not to do it again and if I also do so to admit without modesty the shortcomings of a translation:

> Funerary speech and writing would not follow upon death; they work on life in what we call autobiography. And this takes place between fiction and truth, *Dichtung und Wahrheit.*

An obvious allusion to a distinction between fiction and autobiography that not only remains undecidable but, far more serious, in whose indecidability, as de Man makes clear, it is impossible to *stand*, to maintain oneself in a stable or stationary way. One thus finds oneself in a fatal and double impossibility: the impossibility of deciding, but the impossibility of *remaining* [demeurer] in the undecidable.[2]

I will attempt to speak of this necessary but impossible abidance [*demeurance*] of the abode [*demeure*]. How can one decide what remains abidingly [*à demeure*]? How is one to hear the term—the noun or the verb, the adverbial phrases—"*abode* [la demeure]," "that which *abides* [*ce qui* demeure]," "that which holds *abidingly* [*ce qui se tient* à demeure]," "that by which one must *abide* [*ce qui met* en demeure]"?

Huddled in the shadow of these syllables, dwells [*demeure*]—the troubled grammar of so many sentences. We hear it coming; it is ready for everything.

Goethe, for one, never confused *Dichtung* (equally poorly translated as "poetry") and fiction. *Dichtung* is neither fiction nor poetry. When he means fiction, Goethe says *Fiction*. If, always in irreverent homage to Goethe, *truth* becomes *testimony* here, it is perhaps because, as in *Dichtung und Wahrheit*, it will often be a question today of lies and truth: more precisely, of the biographical or autobiographical truthfulness of a witness who speaks of himself and claims to be recounting not only his life but his death, his quasi-resurrection, a sort of Passion—at the limits of literature. Have no fear, it will not be a question of my autobiography but of another's. The improvised title "Fiction and Testimony" thus seems in its own way "parodistical," to appeal to another of Goethe's terms. Goethe thereby characterized a mode of translation and a period, a way of "appropriating" "a foreign spirit" by "transposing" it into one's own:

> I would call this period parodistical [he says in *The West-Eastern Divan*], taking this word in its purest sense. . . . The French use this procedure in the translation of all poetic works. . . . The Frenchman, just as he adapts all foreign words to his speech, does so for feelings, thoughts and even objects; he demands that a surrogate be found for all foreign fruit at any price, one that has been grown in his own soil.[3]

We are already in the annals of a certain Franco-German border. In Louvain-la-Neuve, in this non-French frontier zone of French-speaking communities, I will begin by staying close to this border, between de Man and Goethe, in order to give proper names to the places and metonymies to the landscape. Everything that I put forward will also be magnetized by a history of the European wars between France and Germany, more precisely and closely related to a certain episode at the end of the last world war and the Nazi Occupation, which still resonates with us today.

Once again Michel Lisse has given us everything and has given himself without reserve. He has offered us hospitality here, at home, in his country and in his university; he has given place to this encounter. And of himself he will have given a title to this encounter, that is, a name, *Passions of Literature*.

Who would dare measure out the gratitude for so many

gifts? They are boundless and without equivalent, thus
without possible return.

But even if from the outset the privileged guest that I
am must give up rendering thanks as much as he should,
he is nonetheless beholden to agree in spirit with the
name chosen by the other, by our host, Michel Lisse, *Passions of Literature*, in order to say what this name gives or
what it gives rise to. The guest must respond to this name,
more than one name, *Passions of Literature*: not respond in
the name of this name or answer for this name, which remains the signature of Michel Lisse, or even bring an answer to the name, but resonate with it, enter into a resonance, a consonance, or a correspondence with *Passions of
Literature*. It cannot be a question of doing this in a way
that would be adequate and adjusted but rather, if possible, in a way that is true [*juste*], according to an affinity.
"True" as is sometimes said in the register of voice or
sound. True and also close—close, that is, in the friendly
relation of a proximity, the vicinity or the borders of an
area, not too far from a threshold, a shore, or a bank.

To attempt this, one would have to hear what the title
Passions of Literature means: first of all what Michel Lisse
wanted it to say, and, more specifically, what he wanted to
have said with these three words or what he meant to say.
Even if this meaning-to-say insists on remaining equivocal, one must nonetheless be ready to secure this equivocation to a shore, to fix or stabilize it within limits that are
assured, abiding [*à demeure*].

But already we are disturbed by the law of number.
There is more than one noun in this name, which a title
always is. The writing plays with the plural and the singular: *Passions of Literature*. Thus there would be more than
one passion but only *one* literature, *literature*—and so an
infinite number of problems amass to cloud our sky. Fur-

thermore the syntax oscillates between more than one
genitive. We can guess that this is not simply for fun, and
if it is a game, it is serious: one will think as readily of the
passions, the many passions *for* literature, devoted to literature, as one will of the passions that a literature, literature
itself, literature in the singular in general, can endure, suffer, accept, or refuse. Literature would thus be the subject
as well as the object of these passions, as well as the can-
vas, or in any case the place, passive and punishable, to
which events supervene: an entire history awaits us. And
first the history of number: if there is only *one* literature,
and if this literature is *literature*, does this mean that it
remains particular or that it is already universal? Is it only
a mode of writing and production specific to the little
thing that is Europe, a barely national piece of European
history and geography? Or else is it already the *Weltliteratur* whose concept was forged by Goethe, yet again, for
his time? Indeed these passages in the *Conversation with
Eckermann* are familiar to us. In them Goethe does not
evoke world literature as a thing of the past, but assigns it
a future task:

> National literature is no longer of importance: it is the time
> for world literature, and all must aid in bringing it about.
> (January 31, 1827)

Furthermore:

> If we have dared proclaim the beginning of a European lit-
> erature, indeed a world literature, this does not merely mean
> that the various nations will take note of one another and
> their creative efforts, for in that sense a world literature has
> been in existence for some time. . . . We mean, rather, that
> living, contemporary writers . . . are becoming acquainted
> and feel the need to take action as a group [*gesellschaftlich*]
> because of inclination and public-spiritedness.[4]

If I insist on these dates, and I often will, it is to recall what a date, that is, the event of signature, inscribes in the relation between fiction and testimony; but it is also because the first decades of the last century situate the historical personalities whose figures, both real and literary, will later pass before us: around Goethe will be Napoleon and then Hegel.

Michel Lisse thought it not unjustified (this is yet another responsibility I leave to him, while thanking him for it) to associate my name with a very beautiful title, *Passions of Literature*. He will thus have encouraged me to confess, if it is not too late, be it in the future anterior, that the name and the thing called "literature" remain for me, to this day, endless enigmas, as much as they remain passions. One might as well say—and for this I also wish to thank him—that by throwing me head first onto literature, Michel Lisse has reminded me that nothing to this day remains as new and as incomprehensible to me, at once very near and very alien, as the thing called literature. Sometimes and especially—I will explain myself— the *name without the thing*.

What is this name? It should at least be emphasized that it belongs, like any name, that is, like any noun, to *language*. Which means, as always—since *language* does not exist, no one has ever encountered it—that it belongs to *a* language. *Literature* is a Latin word. This belonging has never been simple: it is a belonging that travels, emigrates, works, and is translated. The Latin filiation is exported and bastardized beyond its boundaries and affinities but always within the vicinity of its borders. And it does not travel under just any condition. It does not use just any vehicle or figure of transportation. Whatever the diversity of our mother idioms here, when we say *literature*, if it can be supposed that we understand each other,

we speak and make ourselves understood on the basis of a
Latin root, in the constraining hospitality or the violent
reception of a latinity. In all European languages, even
languages in which Latin is not dominant, like English
or German, *literature* remains a Latin word. There is no
thought, no experience, no history of literature as such
and under this name, no world literature, if such a thing
is or remains to come, as Goethe holds somewhat casually,
there is no passion of literature that must not first inherit
what this latinity assumes and thereby show itself capable
of receiving it and, as I would say in French, of suffering
it, which is to accept, to receive, to capacitate, to invite, to
translate into itself, to assimilate, but also to contain, to
keep thus within its boundaries. The consequences of this
are infinite; there is no question of even beginning to lay
them out here.

Yet let us at least take note of this first axiom: everything that does not allow itself to be thus translated or received in this Latin word, everything that precedes or exceeds this history of latinity, cannot seriously and *literally*,
since here it is a matter of the *letter*, be recognized as *literature*. And to take account of the latinity in the modern
institution of literature—which would have to be distinguished from many other proximate things, like tech-
niques, the arts or the fine arts, the other discursive arts
such as poetry, epic or Greek tragedy, belles lettres, etc.—
is not only to take account of Christendom as the Roman
Church, of Roman law and the Roman concept of the
State, indeed of Europe, although this history has counted
greatly in the institution and the constitution of literature,
in its relation to religion and politics. Does there exist, in
the strict and *literal* meaning of the word, something like
literature, like an institution of literature and a right to literature in non–Latin-Roman-Christian culture and, more

generally, although things are indissociable in their history, non-European culture?

Nothing is less certain. I need not call to mind the tragic and geopolitical seriousness of this problem, which, for certain writers, intellectuals and journalists today, becomes a question of life or violent death. This will also be the horizon of this presentation. I cite these three categories (writers, intellectuals, and journalists), as we do in the International Parliament of Writers, in order to associate in a way that is certainly problematic, but as victims of the same murderous persecution, those signatories of public speech who exercise this speech either in the context of what we call literary fiction (Rushdie and all of the writers who not only suffer from an international, supra-state threat of murder but suffer death itself, every day on any street corner, who suffer prison and exile, sometimes inner exile), or in the context of knowledge, information, or testimony, like all intellectuals in general, scientists, professors, or journalists, some of whom are heroes or heroines of testimony today, for example, in my native Algeria. Perhaps it is decent and urgent today, under the title *Passions of Literature*, to begin by saluting those who risk their lives, those who, driven by a certain unconditional imperative of literature and testimony, find themselves exposed to assassins because of this—to murderers whose very crime cannot be determined without taking into account a certain uncomprehending inability to tolerate literature and testimony, as well as their common law. Literature and death, truth and death: this is the subject.

In order to be elaborated, this question concerning the Latin-Europeanness of literature first assumes belief in a rigorous demarcation of what "literature" might mean in a non-figurative and literal sense. This presupposition may resist all elaboration. One would then be faced with a bad question or an impossible question. This would already be, in any case, a question about the possibility of the question, as the question of the *literality of literarity*, insofar as the latter is close in its destiny to the European heritage of Christian Rome. I do not think the abyssal perspective of this question is saturated or perhaps even opened by a historical problematic such as that of Ernst Robert Curtius, however interesting and rich his 1948 *European Literature and the Latin Middle Ages* may be in other respects. It is not certain, for example, that one can follow Curtius with all rigor when he traces the origin of literature back to a Homeric foundation: "The founding hero [*heros ktistes*] of European literature," he says in effect, "is Homer." A formula as contestable, it seems to me, as the one that immediately follows it: "Its last universal author is Goethe."[5] In Greece there is still no project, no social institution, no right, no concept, nor even a word corresponding to what we call, *stricto sensu*, literature. But we will always have the greatest trouble marking out, precisely, the question of this stricture of meaning. To justify my use of this reference for just another moment and to inscribe Goethe, Napoleon, and thus Hegel once more in our excursus, I will remind you that for Curtius—and this assertion seems not to be self-evident—"European literature is coextensive in time with European culture, and therefore embraces a period of some twenty-six centuries (reckoning from Homer to Goethe)" (p. 12). According to Curtius, in order to have access to this literature *as a whole* (he does not say in its *essence* but in its *totality*), one would need to spend time in each of the European literatures, but without settling in them and without nationalism. Literary nationalism would be a modern reaction in Europe, like the awakening of nationalities, to Napoleon's superstate project of hegemony. Whatever one might think of

this interesting hypothesis, one must think about it today
at a time when certain nationalisms are also obscure, indeed obscurantist reactions and resistances to new types of
techno-scientific and capitalist internationalization that
make universalistic or super-state claims which often hide
interests more specific than is generally acknowledged.
Also, without subscribing to them, I will quote several
lines from Curtius. The Weimarian-Roman he sought to
be between the two wars tells us something about the latinity and the history of literary nationalism; in passing, he
also names Rome, Roman citizenship, and, more broadly,
the *romania* to which, as he will show further and abun-
dantly, literature owes so much, both according to the *ro-
manesque* and the *romantic*.[6] Curtius speaks quite calmly
of "grasping [European] literature as a whole," thus in its
totality, without asking himself what we must already pre-
comprehend or problematize of the essence of the literary
before and with a view to approaching, *a fortiori* exhaust-
ing, something like the whole of it. In spite of this theoretical or philosophical limit to Curtius's remarks, one may
find it interesting that he links literary experience to a juridical institution, to acquired rights, and this from the
outset in the Roman figure of citizenship, of *civitas*:

> To see European literature as a whole is possible only after
> one has acquired citizenship in every period from Homer to
> Goethe. . . . One acquires the rights of citizenship in the
> country of European literature only when one has spent
> many years in each of its provinces and has frequently moved
> about from one to another. One is a European when one has
> become a *civis romanus*.

Attentive to the academic, the university, even the de-
partmental causes and effects of this situation, Curtius
goes on:

The division of European literature among a number of un-connected philologies almost completely prevents this. Though "classical" philology goes beyond Augustan litera-ture in research, it seldom does so in teaching. The "mod-ern" philologies are oriented toward the modern "national literatures"—a concept which was first established after the awakening of nationalities under the pressure of the Napo-leonic superstate, which is therefore highly time-conditioned and hence still more obstructive of any view of the whole.

How can one not be tempted to transpose these re-marks to our present day? Against what novel, super-state imperialism do all the forms of nationalism or literary and cultural ethnocentrism react today? And, correspondingly, the interest shown them in the university? In 1947 Cur-tius concludes with optimism: "Specialization has [in the course of the thirties and forties] thus opened the way to a new universalization."[7]

We cannot unfold here all the reasons one might insist on this Roman latinity—or on a certain *universalization* and, as I have tried to show elsewhere,[8] the role played by this universalization, it seems to me, in what happens in what we call by another Latin word, *religion*, in the world today. For the moment, I will note only one of these rea-sons. As if by accident, where nothing is fortuitous, the other word of the title chosen for this encounter, "pas-sions," is just as burdened with Christian latinity.

If one were to unravel the lines of force that semanti-cally traverse the word "passion," one would discover at least *seven* knotted trajectories, which we will have to de-scribe elliptically and at a telegraphic pace. My hypothesis is that these seven trajectories traverse the text *The Instant of My Death*, which Maurice Blanchot published several months ago, and which I will attempt to read with you a little later. I do not know whether this text belongs, purely and properly and strictly and rigorously speaking, to the space of literature, whether it is a fiction or a testimony, and, above all, to what extent it calls these distinctions into question or causes them all to tremble.

Through what place must all these different meanings, these *passionate* trajectories of literature, pass in order to mark there the inscription of their seven seals?

1. "Passion" first implies a history in literature that displays itself *as such* in Christian culture. Literature forced upon the land of Christian passion—more precisely, in its Roman period—linked to the history of rights, of the State, of property, then of modern democracy in its Roman model as well as its Greek one, linked to the history of secularization which takes over from sacrality, before and through the Enlightenment, linked to the history of the novel and of Romanticism.

2. "Passion" also implies the experience of love, of amorous, courtly, knightly, novelistic, romantic passion, where these have become inseparable from the desire to avow, from the confessional testimony and from truthfulness, from *telling the other everything* and *identifying with everything*, with everyone, opening up thus new problems of responsibility before the law and beyond the rights of a state.

3. "Passion" implies finitude, certainly (the whole Kantian moment of the determination of experience as sensibility, space and time, the receptivity of the *intuitus derivativus*), but also a certain passivity in the heteronomic relation to the law and to the other, because this heteronomy is not simply passive and incompatible with freedom and with autonomy, it is a matter of the passivity of passion before or beyond the opposition between passivity and activity. One thinks above all of what Levinas and

Blanchot say of archi-passivity, particularly when Blanchot, unlike Levinas, analyzes the neuter and a certain neutrality of the "narrative voice," a voice without person, without the narrative voice from which the "I" posits and identifies itself.

4. "Passion" also implies liability, that is, imputability, culpability, responsibility, a certain *Schuldigsein*, an originary debt of being-before-the-law.

5. "Passion" implies an engagement that is assumed in pain and suffering, experience without mastery and thus without active subjectivity. Because this passion, which is not active, is not simply passive either, the entire history without history of the middle voice—and perhaps of the neuter of the narrative voice—is opened in passion. If a différance can only be written in the grammar of a certain middle voice, even if it cannot be confined by such a historical grammar, one might be able to reduce "différance" to another name for "passion," as well as to its interpretation, the formalization of this polysemy.

6. In memory of its Christian-Roman meaning, "passion" always implies martyrdom, that is—as its name indicates—testimony. A passion always testifies. But if the testimony always claims to testify in truth to the truth for the truth, it does not consist, for the most part, in sharing a knowledge, in making known, in informing, in speaking true. As a promise to *make truth*, according to Augustine's expression, where the witness must be irreplaceably alone, where the witness alone is capable of dying his own death, testimony always goes hand in hand with at least the *possibility* of fiction, perjury, and lie. Were this possibility to be eliminated, no testimony would be possible any longer; it could no longer have the meaning of testimony. If testimony is passion, that is because it will always *suffer* both having, undecidably, a connection to fiction, perjury, or

lie and never being able or obligated—without ceasing to testify—to become a proof.

7. Finally and above all "passion" implies the endurance of an indeterminate or undecidable limit where something, some X—for example, literature—must bear or tolerate everything, *suffer everything precisely because it is not itself,* because it has no essence but only functions. This at least is the hypothesis I would like to test and submit to your discussion. There is no essence or substance of literature: literature is not. It does not exist. It does not remain at home, *abidingly* [à demeure] in the identity of a nature or even of a historical being identical with itself. It does not maintain itself abidingly [*à demeure*], at least if "abode [*demeure*]" designates the essential stability of a place; it only remains [*demeure*] *where* and *if* "to be abidingly [*être à demeure*]" in some "abiding order [*mise en demeure*]" means something else. The historicity of its experience—for there is one—rests on the very thing no ontology could essentialize. No exposition, no discursive form is intrinsically or essentially *literary* before and outside of the function it is assigned or recognized by a right, that is, a specific intentionality inscribed directly on the social body. The same exposition may be taken to be literary here, in one situation or according to given conventions, and non-literary there. This is the sign that literarity is not an intrinsic property of this or that discursive event. Even where it seems to *reside* [demeurer], literature remains an unstable function, and it depends on a precarious juridical status. Its passion consists in this—that it receives its determination from something other than itself. Even when it harbors the unconditional right to say anything, including the most savage antinomies, disobedience itself, its *status* is never assured or guaranteed permanently [*à demeure*], at home, in the inside of an "at

home." This contradiction is its very existence, its ecstatic process. Before coming to writing, literature depends on reading and the right conferred on it by an experience of reading. One can read the same text—which thus never exists "in itself"—as a testimony that is said to be serious and authentic, or as an archive, or as a document, or as a symptom—or as a work of literary fiction, indeed the work of a literary fiction that simulates all of the positions that we have just enumerated. For literature can say anything, accept anything, receive anything, suffer anything, and simulate everything; it can even feign a trap, the way modern armies know how to set false traps; these traps pass themselves off as real traps and trick the machines designed to detect simulations under even the most sophisticated camouflage.

Why insist on law to such an extent? In our European juridical tradition, testimony should remain unrelated to literature and especially, in literature, to what presents itself as fiction, simulation, or simulacra, which is not all literature. When a testifying witness, whether or not he is explicitly under oath, without being able or obligated to prove anything, appeals to the faith of the other by engaging himself to tell the truth—no judge will accept that he should shirk his responsibility ironically by declaring or insinuating: what I am telling you here retains the status of a literary fiction. And yet, if the testimonial is by law irreducible to the fictional, there is no testimony that does not structurally imply in itself the possibility of fiction, simulacra, dissimulation, lie, and perjury—that is to say, the possibility of literature, of the innocent or perverse literature that innocently plays at perverting all of these distinctions. If this possibility that it seems to prohibit were effectively excluded, if testimony thereby became proof, information, certainty, or archive, it would lose its function as testimony. In order to remain testimony, it must therefore allow itself to be haunted. It must allow itself to be parasitized by precisely what it excludes from its inner depths, the *possibility*, at least, of literature. We will try to remain [*demeurer*] on this undecidable limit. It is a chance and a threat, a resource both of testimony and of literary fiction, law and non-law, truth and non-truth, veracity and lie, faithfulness and perjury.

Thus an impossible limit. Untenable. This limit permanently [*à demeure*] swears testimony to secrecy; it enjoins testimony to remain [*demeurer*] secret, even where it makes manifest and public. I can only testify, in the strict sense of the word, from the instant when no one can, in my place, testify to what I do. What I testify to is, at that very instant, my secret; it remains reserved for me. I must be able to keep secret precisely what I testify to; it is the condition of the testimony in a strict sense, and this is why one will never be able to demonstrate, in the sense of a theoretical proof or a determinate judgment, that a perjury or lie has in fact taken place. Even an admission will not be enough.

By tying testimony both to the secret and to the instant, by saying at this very instant *at this very instant*, I would like to announce a singular testimonial alliance of the secret and the instant, namely, that which, in the indivisible unicity of the instant, is temporalized without being temporalized *permanently* [à demeure]. The question that immediately arises is one of knowing whether a secret testimony is impossible. In principle, to testify—not being a witness but testifying, attesting, "bearing witness"—is always to render public. The value of publicity, that is, of broad daylight (phenomenality, openness, popularity, *res publica*, and politics) seems associated in some essential way with that of testimony. The idea of a secret testimony seems thus a contradiction in terms. Especially when the experience of the secret itself implies some inner witness, some third party in oneself that one calls to witness. Testifying to a secret, attesting to there being some secret without revealing the heart of the secret, is a critical possibility to which Blanchot, for example, has been very attentive, as he has been to the possibility of testifying to the absence of attestation when we feel it a duty to attest before the other to an attestation's not being possible—and that there is here a secret to keep or a secret that one cannot not keep: the avowal of a secret having remained secret.

In *The Step Not Beyond*, Blanchot associates attestation with the Neuter, the singular place of a passion beyond the opposition of passive and active:

> ♦ The Neuter, the gentle prohibition against dying, there where, from threshold to threshold, eye without gaze, silence carries us into the proximity of the distant. Word still to be spoken beyond the living and the dead, *testifying for the absence of attestation.*[9]

This sentence, as is often the case, tells of the double suffering of the same passion, the passion of death in life, not only the impossible death, but the dying prohibited, the "gentle prohibition against dying." The last words (*testifying for the absence of attestation*) are italicized. They resonate in what is perhaps a contrasting echo with the "no one / testifies for the / witness" (*Niemand / zeugt für den / Zeugen*) of Celan, who had died shortly before. No one testifies *for* the witness but "speech . . . *testifying* for the *absence of attestation,*" with a "for" whose rich equivocation remains ungraspable ("in the place of," "on behalf of," "destined for"). Further, in the same book, three exchanges follow one upon the other without connecting:

♦ Grafted onto every word: the neuter.

♦ *It is as if he had said to him, saying it in such a friendly way: friendship withdraws from us.*

♦ *Enlaced, separated: witnesses without attestation, coming toward us, also coming toward each other, at the detour of time that they were called upon to make turn.*

Where does this turning point of time turn? What does this detour, this turning away or turning of time have to do with the test of the instant, as instant of the secret? To testify to a secret, what does this mean? How can one testify to what, in principle, is destined to refuse itself to testimony? The engagement to keep secret is a testimony. The secret assumes not only that there should be some witness, be it, as one says, to share in a secret, but it assumes that the testimony will not simply consist in knowing or making known a secret, in sharing it, but in engaging oneself, in an implicit or explicit manner, to keeping the secret. In other words, the experience of the secret is, however contradictory this may seem, a testimonial experience. And consequently the question of number arises: the question of the one, the two, the three, and the immense question of the third, of the witness as third party (*testis, terstis*). What is the third party to a secret? What is the place of the witness? Is the witness the one who takes part in a secret dual, or is the witness not already a third in the secret?

Testimony seems to presuppose the instance of the instant that, at that very instant, however, it destroys. It destroys it as if it were destroying its own condition of possibility.

For to testify is always *on the one hand* to do it *at present*—the witness must be present at the stand himself, without technical interposition. In the law, the testimonial tends, without being able to succeed in this altogether, to exclude all technical agency. One cannot send a cassette to testify in one's place. One must oneself be present, raise one's hand, speak in the first person and in the present, and one must do this in order to testify to a present, to an indivisible moment, that is, at a certain point to a moment assembled at the tip of an instantaneousness which must resist division. If that to which I testify is divisible, if the moment in which I testify is divisible, if my attestation is divisible, at that moment it is no longer reliable, it no longer has the value of truth, reliability, or veracity that it claims absolutely. Consequently, for testimony there *must* be the instant.

And yet, *on the other hand*, this condition of possibility is destroyed by the testimony itself. Ocular, auditory, tactile, any sensory perception of the witness must be an experience. As such, a constituting synthesis entails time and thus does not limit itself to the instant. The moment one is a witness and the moment one attests, *bears witness*, the instant one gives testimony, there must also be a temporal sequence—sentences, for example—and, above all, these sentences must promise their own repetition and thus their own quasi-technical reproducibility. When I commit myself to speaking the truth, I commit myself to repeating the same thing, an instant later, two instants later, the next day, and for eternity, in a certain way. But this repetition carries the instant outside of itself. Consequently the instant is instantaneously, *at this very instant*, divided, destroyed by what it nonetheless makes possible—testimony. How is it that the instant makes testimony both possible and impossible at the same time? It is these questions, thus stated in a formal, elliptical or shrouded way, that we will slowly try to bring out.

~

This instant, at this very instant, I am speaking French, we are speaking French. This is a testimony. And this in-

stant, as I am saying this, I pass and I have already passed
from *I* to *you*. I am speaking French, we are speaking
French. I can only say I am speaking French if it is assumed, as soon as I speak, this instant, in this very instant,
that someone here, now, at least someone is able to understand this language that I call and is called French, and
is able to form from the outset a *we* with the one who is
speaking here this instant, with me, consequently. Thus:
we are immediately more than one, as soon as *I* or an *I*
speaks, of course, but in any case from the instant I am
speaking French and say that I am speaking French. I
am not only speaking French, I am saying that I am speaking French. I am saying it in French. Even if—hypothetically—no one here this instant spoke French, no one but
me, well even then, my speech act in French would nonetheless continue to assume someone, however indeterminate or distant he might be, someone who could understand what I am saying and who would form a *we* with
me, someone who commits himself to forming a *we* with
me—even if I were alone in speaking French here or even
if I were simply speaking alone. This "we" without which
there would be no testimony, this indeterminate "we" does
not necessarily presuppose any agreement with what I am
saying, any sympathy, any community, any consensus of
any kind, except a minimal way of being, let us say, of an
understanding with the other, with me here in the language, the instant it is being spoken, was being spoken,
and the instant I say, "This instant I am speaking French,
we are speaking French," and the instant I use—and I
will already make note of it in order to return to it later at
greater length—a very idiomatic expression, almost untranslatable, namely *à l'instant.* Just as the noun, verb, or
adverbial phrases *la demeure, demeurer, à demeure, en demeure* will remain untranslatable in their usage. This id-

iom can no longer be erased; we will experience this, in the test of testimony, of the secret and of responsibility.

A priori or originary in the play of enunciation, as one says, where it is only or at the very least a question of an understanding of the language, such an implication of the "we"—the "we" as a sharing of the idiom and co-responsibility for linguistic competence, so to speak—testifies to an essence of testimony. There could be no attestation without it. There could be no witness—not only no witness who is present and one who perceives as witness but no witness who attests, who *bears witness*—without speech act, of course, but above all without someone who can be assumed to have at least a sufficient mastery of the language. This is an endless problem, a dramatic problem whose critical, political and juridical dimensions it is not necessary to underline. To what extent can this competence be shared? How and on the basis of what metalinguistic criteria can it be evaluated? The analysis of this mastery would call for infinite refinements. In any case, the juridical concept of attestation implies a sufficient mastery of the language, however problematic this concept may remain. The same concept must at the same time assume an addressee capable of the same mastery, that is, of hearing and translating in univocal fashion, without misunderstanding, in the same proportion—but what does "proportion" mean here, where it is a question of understanding the language—and of saying or inferring "we," even if the addressee in question should contest, deny, suspect, disbelieve the *content* of what is said. Furthermore, he would have to begin by understanding in order to begin contesting the attestation. And, above all, he would have to be certain of the distinction between a testimony and a fiction of testimony: for example, between a discourse that is put forward seriously, in good faith, under oath, and a text that lies, pretends to tell the truth, or goes so far as to simulate the oath itself, either with a view to deceiving or with a view to producing a literary work, or, further, by confusing the limit between the two in order to dissolve the criteria of responsibility. It is this possibility, a possibility that is always open—and which must remain open for better and for worse—that we are going to discuss. This is where a passion of literature would take place, this is where it would have one of its places, if not its proper place.

Even perjury, in the case of false testimony—false testimony is perjury—even a lie presupposes the structure "I am speaking," "we are speaking the same language." There would be no lie otherwise, and this sharing of competence even reveals the condition of the lie. One must speak the same language to the point of the worst misunderstanding and in view of the interruption of the *we*, in view of the most radical, war-like rupture, dissociative of the "we"—in the lie, in perjury, in deception, in false testimony, which is not, I will remind you, testimony that is false. A testimony can be false, that is, mistaken, without being false testimony—that is, without implicating perjury, lie, a deliberate intention to deceive. False testimony assumes this agreement in language. I could not lie if I did not presuppose that the other understands what I am saying to him *as* I am saying it to him, *as* I want to say it to him. There is no lie otherwise. I tell you this, you believe it, you understand what I mean, and you must understand exactly what I mean for me to be able to lie or perjure myself. Thus I can only lie to someone who hears me, who understands me, who understands me in my language the instant I am speaking to him or to someone of whom it is assumed that his competence rigorously equals, indeed matches my own: linguistic, rhetorical, I would even say pragmatic competence, for it is not only a matter of words and discourse—one can lie wordlessly—it is a matter of all the codes involved in a pragmatics, of the gestures of the body that accompany, surround, and determine a speech act, indeed any given speech. It may be a matter of the gaze, the hand, any silent movement in the space of the so-called body proper. But also, above all, the pragmatic conventions that surround a discursive act. Let us take the example of two perfectly identical discourses, identical down to their commas: the one can be lying if it presents itself as a serious and non-fictitious address to the other, but the other (the same in its content) is no longer lying if it surrounds itself with the distinctive signs of literary fiction, for example, by being published in a collection that clearly says: this is literature, the narrator is not the author, no one has committed himself here to telling the truth before the law, thus no one can be accused of lying. But is this limit ever so clear and can it remain that way?

This very complex statement ("this instant, at this very instant I am speaking French, we are speaking French") constitutes a testimony whose layered structure would require lengthy analyses. It is an exemplary testimony for many reasons. First, like any testimony, it says something, it describes something, it makes known, it brings to knowledge, it informs; one could almost say that it recounts, it gives account: here it is, I am telling you that I am speaking French. I testify that I am speaking French and I inform the addressees who understand the language I am speaking of this. But the fact that they understand the language I am speaking does not prevent one from dissociating the instant and the instance of this statement into two heterogeneous functions: on the one hand, they learn that I am speaking French, and they understand this simply insofar as they understand French. But on the other hand, at the same time, they understand the content, namely, that I am telling them I am speaking French. I could say to them in French: I am speaking English, and there would also be a content, it would be a false testimony, but it would be a content distinguishable from the act of testifying. In the statement with which I say "I am speaking French" there are thus these two heterogeneous strata, even if they come together in a single occurrence that has become in some sense its own homonym. Thus I testify that I am speaking French, and I inform the addressees who understand the language I am speaking of this. This is the first condition of testimony. Next, the statement does this, as all testimony must, in the first person. A testimony is always given in the first person. And here it is given twice in the first person, because I said: I am speaking French, we are speaking French—first person singular, first person plural. Finally, and this is what is most important to me here and what will bring us back to the bifid structure in some sense of all testimony: this statement is not merely recounting, telling, informing, describing, remarking—it does this as well—it does what it says at this very instant; it cannot essentially be reduced to a relationship, to a narrative or descriptive relation; it is an act. The essence of testimony cannot necessarily be reduced to narration, that is, to descriptive, informative relations, to knowledge or to narrative; it is first a present act. When he testifies the martyr does not tell a story, he offers himself. He testifies to his faith by offering himself or offering his life or his body, and this act of testimony is not only an engagement, but his passion does not refer to anything other than its present moment.

The *Discourse on Method* provides a test of this linguistic situation. In it Descartes gives the reasons why he writes in French, one being his desire to be understood by women and not only by those "more subtle" ("I wanted it such that even women would be able to understand something, and yet for those more subtle still to find matter enough to occupy their minds"). A cunning strategy, that of Descartes, at a time when the hospitality offered a certain French community was not limited to the official francophone countries, like this country today, but rather extended to more than one European court. Yet when the *Discours de la méthode* was later translated into Latin, the translator simply skipped over this passage. By that time he judged it to be useless or unintelligible, French having disappeared and with it the performative "I am writing in French," the theoretical explanation that, in the same language, formed one body with it also had to be passed over in silence.

Let us move on now. This instant, in saying that in this instant I am speaking French and that we are speaking French, I am not only testifying in French to the fact that I am testifying in French. I am signing it untranslatably or, in any case, in such a way that its translation without remainder seems difficult if not impossible. And here we rediscover our initial worry: not only "What is the instant?" but "What does *instant* mean in French?" And what does *instance*—from which it is inseparable—mean, in the same language?

It is already difficult to say what these words mean in French, or in a language with a Latin filiation. This difficulty is increased the instant one takes into account that in English, for example, "instant" and "instance" have very different meanings. The apparent homonyms have very different meanings. One knows this, one recognizes this; even so, one has to be cultivated enough, informed, competent, sufficiently educated to do so and to testify to it.

This is the whole problem of the relation between a supposed culture, a competence without criteria, and the apti-
tude to bear witness. For the witness must both conform to
given criteria and at the same time invent, in quasi-poetic
fashion, the norms of his attestation. The stakes are enormous for the social, political, or juridical order of educa-
tion, as for the exercise of citizenship. And one must know
how to make oneself heard. Must one know how to write?
This is yet another problem. If one takes the examples of
religious testimony, of revelation or sacred attestation, the
dissociation between speech and writing may become quite
acute. Mahomet did not know how to write, supposedly,
which did not prevent him from speaking and testifying
through his speech. This said, what is indispensable, even
for a witness who does not know how to write, in the common and trivial sense of the word, is that he be capable of
inscribing, tracing, repeating, remembering, performing
the acts of synthesis that writing is. Thus he needs some
writing power, at the very least, some possibility of tracing
or imprinting in a given element. The difficulty increases
when one notices—the example of English seems simpler
because there are many anglophones among us—that "instance" leads us more in the direction of exemplarity: "instance" is an example, and exemplarity names a concept essential to the problematic of testimony. A witness and a
testimony must always be exemplary. They must first be
singular, whence the necessity of the instant: I am the only
one to have seen this unique thing, the only one to have
heard or to have been put in the presence of this or that, at
a determinate, indivisible instant; and you must believe me
because you must believe me—this is the difference, essential to testimony, between belief and proof—you must
believe me because I am irreplaceable. When I testify, I am
unique and irreplaceable. And at the very tip of this irre-

placeability, this unicity, once again, there is the instant. Even if we have been several to participate in an event, to have been present at a scene, the witness can only testify when he asserts that he was in a unique place and where he could testify to this and that in a here-now, that is, in a pointed instant that precisely supports this exemplarity. The example is not substitutable; but at the same time the same aporia always remains: this irreplaceability must be exemplary, that is, replaceable. The irreplaceable must allow itself to be replaced on the spot. In saying: I swear to tell the truth, where I have been the only one to see or hear and where I am the only one who can attest to it, this is true to the extent that anyone who *in my place*, at that instant, would have seen or heard or touched the same thing and could repeat exemplarily, universally, the truth of my testimony. The exemplarity of the "instant," that which makes it an "instance," if you like, is that it is singular, like any exemplarity, singular *and* universal, singular *and* universalizable. The singular must be universalizable; this is the testimonial condition. Simultaneously, at the same instant, in the "I swear, you must believe me," I am claiming, I am demanding, I am postulating the possible and necessary universalization of this singularity: anyone who *in my place*, etc., would confirm my testimony, which is thus both infinitely secret and infinitely public; and this is why I commit myself in advance to repeating, and I begin by repeating. What I say for the first time, if it is a testimony, is already a repetition, at least a repeatability; it is already an iterability, more than once at once, more than an instant in one instant, at the same time; and that being the case, the instant is always divided at its very point, at the point of its writing. It is always on the verge [*en instance*] of being divided, whence the problem of idealization. To the extent that it is repeatable, the singular instant becomes an

ideal instant. The root of the testimonial problem of *technē*
is to be found here. The technical reproducibility is excluded from testimony, which always calls for the presence
of the live voice in the first person. But from the moment
that a testimony must be able to be repeated, *technē* is ad-
mitted; it is introduced where it is excluded. For this, one
need not wait for cameras, videos, typewriters, and com-
puters. As soon as the sentence is repeatable, that is, from
its origin, the instant it is pronounced and becomes intel-
ligible, thus idealizable, it is already instrumentalizable and
affected by technology. And virtuality. It is thus the very
instance of the instant that seems to become exemplary:
exemplary in the very place where it seems unique and irreplaceable, under the seal of unicity. And it is perhaps
here, with the technological both as ideality and prosthetic
iterability, that the possibility of fiction *and* lie, simulacrum *and* literature, that of the right to literature insinu-
ates itself, at the very origin of truthful testimony, autobiography in good faith, sincere confession, as their essential
compossibility.

Insofar as it takes on the responsibility of saying what is
true, testimony is thus always a matter of instant and instance or exemplary "instance." In more than one language. In more than one language, not only because I said
instant and "instance" (I could have said *Inständigkeit* and
engaged in a lengthy reading of Heidegger; this will be for
another time) but in more than one language because if it
is already audible at the threshold of the most idiomatic,
the most untranslatable singularity, this appeal to universalization is an appeal to translation. As idiomatic as it
must remain, a testimony claims to be translatable. "I am
speaking French," this instant, as untranslatable as it may
be, can only be a testimony purveyor of truth if its trans-
latability is also promised. One must be able to translate

this sentence. This appeal to instantaneousness as *stigmē*, as singular point of time, thus conveys the aporia of testimony. Besides its juridical-administrative meaning, in French *instance* also means, among other things, "imminence." We are now standing in this imminence—we will experience it in an instant.

~

To test this exemplarity of the instance and the disturbing complicity between fiction and testimony, I will appeal to the example of an enormous text by Maurice Blanchot. It takes up just a few pages and appeared less than a year ago. *The Instant of My Death* will not simply illustrate what we are saying. I want to follow it to the point where, taking us beyond all the categories upon which we too easily rely, it helps us to render them problematic, fragile, uneasy.

It will be a question of autobiography. Is this only because a certain "I" speaks of itself, recounts itself or confesses itself as another? We will analyze the strange position of the narrating *ego* in this narrative. No, it will be a question of autobiography to the extent that it presents itself as testimony. In essence a testimony is always autobiographical: it tells, in the first person, the sharable and unsharable secret of what happened to me, to me, to me alone, the absolute secret of what I was in a position to live, see, hear, touch, sense, and feel. But the classical concept of attestation, like that of autobiography, seems by law to exclude both fiction and art, as soon as the truth, all the truth and nothing but the truth, is owing. By law, a testimony must not be a work of art or a fiction. In testimony, *Wahrheit* excludes *Dichtung*. I will recall in passing that the subtitle or surtitle of *Dichtung und Wahrheit* is *Aus meinen Leben*: "of my life," "drawn from my life," "based on my life," "from my life"—*of* as *from*. One often translates this as "Recollections of My Life."

As an epigraph to this reading, one could inscribe a thousand earlier texts of Blanchot that seem always to have announced *The Instant of My Death*. I will choose only one. It gives the condition under which autobiographical testimony presents itself "in the manner of a work of art," in particular (this is why I am choosing it in honor of my hosts [*hôtes*], of you yourselves, of our hosts or of the guests [*hôtes*] that we are for one another here in different senses), this fragment names a certain *hospitality*, the place of the reader as another and of the other as a guest/host [*hôte*] to whom this autobiographical witness and artist confesses *nothing*—in short, gives nothing, nothing to be known except his death, his inexistence, addressing himself to another in whom he trusts the instant that he confides *everything as nothing* to him.

The hospitality of death itself. This is a definition in *The Writing of the Disaster*. Here, in the book that bears this name, one of the diamonded statements, stamped with a black diamond like a musical note (in plainsong, the diamond is half a breve, it says the *other* as *guest/host* [hôte] for an autobiography, a *hostobiography* which, under certain conditions (the surviving in suicide) advances in the manner of a work of art. Not as a work of art, but rather—which is not altogether the same thing—*in the manner of a work of art*, perhaps by pretending to be a fiction and thus as the fiction of a fiction, as if it were a matter of taking responsibility by no longer answering for it and of manifesting the truth by leaving one the responsibility of receiving it through lie or fiction.

> ♦ To write one's autobiography, in order either to confess or to engage in self-analysis or in order to expose oneself to the gaze of all, *in the manner of a work of art*, is perhaps to seek to survive, but through a perpetual suicide—*total insofar as fragmentary death.*

> To write (of) oneself is to cease to be, in order to confide in a guest/host [hôte]—the other, a reader—who will henceforth have as charge and as life nothing but your inexistence.[10]

This allusion to the "total insofar as fragmentary death" already places us in literature. It recalls what Goethe, again, already said of literature, even if it be *Weltliteratur*, namely, that it was "the fragment of fragments."

At this instant *The Instant of My Death* thus promises us a narrative or a testimony—signed by someone who tells us in many ways and according to every possible tense: *I am* dead, or *I will be* dead in an instant, or an instant ago *I was* going to be dead. Someone intends to speak, to speak to us, not only *of* his death, but *of* his death in the sense of the Latin *de*, in the sense of *from* his death: not *aus meinen Leben* as in *Dichtung und Wahrheit*, of my life from my life, but *on the contrary*, one might say, *from* my death, *from* the place and *from* the taking-place, better yet, from the *having-taken-place*, already, of my death.

Allow me to call to mind an essential kind of generality: is the witness not always a survivor? This belongs to the structure of testimony. One testifies only when one has lived longer than what has come to pass. One can take examples as tragic or full of pathos as the survivors of the death camps. But what ties testimony to *survivance* remains a universal structure and covers the whole elementary field of experience. The witness is a survivor, the third party, the *terstis* as *testis* and *superstes*, the one who survives. This surviving speech must be as exemplarily irreplaceable as the instance of the instant from which it speaks, the instant of death as irreplaceable, as "my death," on the subject of which no one other than the dying person can testify. I am the only one who can testify to my death—on the condition that I survive it.

But at this instant, the same instant, good common

sense reminds us: from the viewpoint of common sense,
I certainly cannot testify to my death—by definition. I
cannot say, according to common sense, I should not be
able to say: I died or I am dead. Much has been written,
I too have written on occasion, about the impossible possibility of the statement "I am dead," on the expression
of Valdemar, who wakes up to say "I am dead," this "I
am" of the "I am dead" that is both present and part of a
past perfect. If there is a place or an instance in which
there is no witness for the witness or where no one is witness for the witness, it would be death. One cannot testify for the witness who testifies to his death, but, inversely, I cannot, I should not be able to, testify to my
own death, only to the imminence of my death, to its *instance* as *deferred imminence.* I can testify to the imminence of my death. And in fact, we recalled earlier that
instance (where the French word seems untranslatable,
like the testimony of my death) could signify more than
one thing: not only, in the language of the law, the place
of administrative or juridical authority, the place of a verdict, such as a magistrates' court or the proceedings of a
court of justice, but also imminence and deferral, the
added delay preceding the "thing" that is pending [*en instance*] because it cannot be long in coming, to the point
of being *on the point* of arriving. One also says of a letter
that is being held in general delivery that it is "on hold
[*en instance*]" awaiting delivery, and this sufferance of the
letter is also the passion of the being in abeyance [*de l'être
en instance*]. But what can an instant in abeyance [*un instant en instance*] be then? Yet here is the last word of the
text before us:

> The instant of my death henceforth always in abeyance [*en
> instance*].

Whoever is even a bit familiar with the work of Blanchot knows well that the themes of testimony and the absence of attestation, the impossible dying, the imminence of an impossible dying, the impossible necessary death have not lain in wait for *The Instant of My Death*. "An impossible necessary death" is already *The Writing of the Disaster*. Death is not impossible *but* necessary, nor is death impossible *and* necessary, no, the impossible and the necessary are neither connected by an "and" nor disconnected by a "but." Death is, in a single stroke, the "impossible necessary," where impossibility and necessity both reciprocally refer to and co-implicate each other, both subject and attribute each to the other abidingly [*à demeure*]. Following a colon, Blanchot wonders about these two words that form without forming an odd phrase. There is nothing fortuitous in the fact that this questioning mentions "fiction" and the fiction specific to an author:

♦ an Impossible necessary death: why do these words [impossible necessary death, thus]—and the *unexperienced experience* to which they refer—escape comprehension? Why this collision, this refusal? Why erase them by making them into a *fiction specific to an author*?[11]

What runs through this testimony of fiction is thus the singular concept of an "unexperienced experience." Nothing seems more absurd to common sense, in effect, than an unexperienced experience. But whoever does not try to think and read the part of fiction and thus of literature that is ushered in by such a phrase in even the most authentic testimony will not have begun to read or hear Blanchot. This holds for the majority of his political prosecutors, among others. They are certainly not wrong to be interested in Blanchot's politics, on the contrary, but they

should at least begin by reading him and learning to read
him—in particular, where fiction plays such a dangerous
and disconcerting game with the seriousness or veracity
of testimony. If a witness came to the stand, swore to tell
the truth, and then broke into a discourse about the "unexperienced" in his "experience"—well, one could bet
that the judge would no longer take him seriously, would
either accuse him of perjury and turn him over to the police or dismiss him as irresponsible and not knowing or
believing what he says and have him examined by a psy-
chiatrist right away: in this way one could bring in all the
characters, the "police commissioner" and the doctors
(the oculist or the "specialists in mental illness") whose
authority [*instances*] is mentioned at the end of *The Madness of the Day*, a narrative which is close in many regards
to *The Instant of My Death* and which, after all, perhaps
recounts the same thing. The literary critic or the university professor who would be Blanchot's political prosecu-
tor and who does not take it upon himself to begin by
reading and thinking, with Blanchot, about these strange
things in the entanglement of testimony and fiction,
would in the best-case scenario (the hypothesis of the
greatest dignity and the least "good conscience") be in the
position of the police commissioner who is on the side of
the doctor—both of whom are already staged in the literature about which they claim to reach a diagnosis or to
pass judgment. Police commissioners and specialists in
mental illness are needed; but they are defined, in their
authority [*instance*], their position, their right, their status, as the very ones who rely on a naive concept of testimony, requiring a narrative of common sense when its
madness is put to the test of the impossible. Incompetent
in their supposed competence, precisely. They confess, in
short, without knowing it, or rather they reveal a symp-

tom: they neither read nor think about what they judge
and diagnose.

~

In France, in French, in a community of French speak-
ers—for it is of this and from here that we are speaking,
just as we are speaking of a war at this border when the
line of demarcation also passes through occupied France,
in France and in French, from the instant there is instantaneity and also the instance, the juridical instance and the
instance as imminence, the instance of "on the point of."
Instantaneity is only the last instance when it is a matter of
"dying." The following is also written in *The Writing of the
Disaster*:

> ♦ Dying is, speaking absolutely, the incessant imminence
> whereby life nonetheless endures by desiring. The immi-
> nence of what has always already taken place.[12]

"The imminence of what has always already taken
place": this is an *unbelievable* tense. It seems to deport
what has always, from all time, already taken place toward
the coming of the to-come. Indeed one must say *unbelievable*, for insofar as all testimony essentially appeals to a
certain system of belief, to faith without proof, to the act
of faith summoned by a kind of transcendental oath, well,
faith in a temporal order, in a certain commonsense or-
dering of time, is what guarantees the everyday concept,
especially the juridical concept and the dominant concept
of attestation in European culture, that in which literature
has been established, thus confirming or disturbing the
very order that conveys it. Imminence, the instance of
what will already have taken place, will be in question in
The Instant of My Death. Death will come, there is a suspension, a last suspensive delay, an interruption of the
death sentence. But what will come, what is coming at

me, this is what will already have taken place: death has already taken place. I can testify to it, because it has already taken place. Yet this past, to which I testify, namely, my death itself, has never been present.

Another sentence of *The Writing of the Disaster* says the same—in short, the same thing otherwise. If I quote once again, but less often than I might, these texts prior to *The Instant of My Death*, it is to mark—although it is altogether new, novel, singular and disturbing—that this last narrative also marks the repetition of what will have always already been said in Blanchot's earlier texts, giving them to us to be read again, confirming and thereby relaunching the singular anachrony of time of which we are speaking, and of which the text speaks in the first place:

I die before being born

says another sentence in *The Writing of the Disaster*. As impossible as it may be to attest to this, as it would be to a present that should normally have presented itself, death has already taken place, and I can testify to it. Blanchot attested to an earlier death, long before *The Instant of My Death*; he did so in an informal address that is almost monological or soliloquized, addressed to itself: "you are dead" are the last words before the epilogue of *The Instant of My Death*, a "you are dead" ("I am alive. No, you are dead") which reports (the constative of a death report), judges or performatively threatens, accuses, judges (you are condemned to death, die: a death sentence, a sentencing, a verdict of the judge or doctor) and threatens as one apostrophes an enemy by telling him, "Put your hands up, you are dead." Yet these last words, these next to last words of *The Instant of My Death*, "you are dead," were already to be found, more than ten years earlier, in *The Writing of the Disaster* as the very definition of disaster, or rather, of the writing-of-disaster, as an undecomposable phrase that destines writing for disaster and disaster for writing.

♦ Dying means: you are dead already, in an immemorial past, by a death that was not your own, which you have thus neither known nor lived, but under the threat of which you believe you are called to live; you await it henceforth in the future, constructing a future to make it possible at last, possible as something that will take place and will belong to the realm of experience.

To write is no longer to put in the future a death always already past, but to accept that one must endure it without making it present and without making oneself present to it; it is to know that death has taken place even though it has not been experienced, and to recognize it in the forgetting that it leaves, whose traces, which can be erased, call upon one *to exempt oneself from the cosmic order*, where disaster makes the real impossible and desire undesirable.

This uncertain death, always anterior, the attestation to a past without present, is never individual, just as it overflows the whole.[13]

By speaking of a death that, in order to be irreplaceable and because it is unique, is not even individual—"never individual," he says—Blanchot puts forward a statement that would appear troublesome even to the *Jemeinigkeit*, the "mine every time," which according to Heidegger essentially characterizes a *Dasein* that announces itself to itself in its own being-for-death.

~

Let us come now to *The Instant of My Death*. In it Blanchot recounts otherwise how at the end of the war—and we know this precisely from testimonies, different and varied testimonies—during an episode recounted to us by the text, the author himself was stopped by the Germans. He was placed before a wall to be executed. He was going to be executed and death had already arrived, had already been decided, decreed; death was imminent and inescapable in a certain way, just as it was for Dostoyevsky—we will return to the specter of Dostoyevsky later on, for there is a Russian dimension to this story. At this instant, he escapes execution. He slowly gets away, without fleeing, under conditions that are barely believable. He is telling the story, and it happened. At the risk once again of being violent toward Blanchot—who is discretion itself—I will dare to do what I think I have never done before in my life, but what I judge to be necessary here for the reading I would like to attempt, in order to place an allegedly non-literary and non-fictional testimony in relation to a testimony presented in a literary mode. I will therefore quote the fragment of a letter I received from Blanchot last summer, just a year ago, almost to the day, as if today were the anniversary of the day on which I received this letter, after July 20. Here are its first two lines; they speak of the anniversary of a death that took place without taking place. Blanchot wrote me thus, on July 20, first making note of the anniversary date:

> July 20. Fifty years ago, I knew the happiness of nearly being shot to death.

Like this sentence, this letter does not belong to what we call literature. It testifies, as I am testifying here, in a space supposedly unrelated to fiction in general and the institution of literature in particular. But it says the same thing. It testifies to the reality of the event that seems to form the referent of this literary narrative entitled *The Instant of My Death* and published as literary fiction. As we will see, the text testifies to this strange event in a way that is abyssal, elliptical, paradoxical, and, for that matter [*au demeurant*], undecidable.

We have only discussed the title, *The Instant of My Death*. The entire narrative is but a gloss, a justification and expansion of a title that speaks of itself and for itself.

The first words, *incipit*: "JE ME SOUVIENS d'un jeune homme; I REMEMBER a young man." The "je" that says "je me" is not the real author, of course, but a narrator; we know that as soon as we approach this book as a literary thing with fictional status. The self-reference of the "I" that does not speak in Blanchot's voice presents a narrator. This narrator is engaging in an act of memory. He attests to remembering someone, someone else, a young man. Already from the *incipit* there is a division of the subject. And more than one age. Aside from the presumed author, *there are two*, and number, two instances: the narrator declaring that he remembers another, and the other; until the end, the story announces itself as the narrative of what happened to a third person, as what happens to him, "he," the third party. Until the end, until the "I" returns at the end, and the "you." This passage to a "he," in the third person, the young man, of course signifies the discretion of the literary process, the ellipsis of someone who is not going to put himself forward and expose himself indiscreetly. This is the difference between the letter I received last July and this literary fiction. But the third also marks a division introduced into the identity of Maurice Blanchot, as into the identities of the narrator and of the young man of whom the narrator speaks. Such a division dissociates them within themselves starting from the event, that is, the event of death that happened to him, that happened to both of them—for in a certain way both die—but also, if I can say this, to both of them plus one, to all three of them: Blanchot, the narrator, and the young man. Death happened to him-them, it arrived *to* divide the subject of this story in some sense: it arrived at this division, but it did not arrive except insofar as it arrived (managed) thus to divide the subject.

> I REMEMBER a young man—a man still young—prevented from dying by death itself.[14]

By this we understand that what happens to him is not the dying, it is not dying. It is not dying but following a verdict that is an order to die: die, you are dead, you are going to die. The order to die comes to prevent him from dying ("prevented from dying by death itself"), and the testimony will in some sense recount this division, in its dividend and its divisor. From dying, he is prevented by death itself. This singular division is the true theme of a testimony that will testify, in sum, to an "unexperienced experience": being "prevented from dying by death itself—and perhaps the error of injustice."

One could spend years on this sentence. On the *perhaps*, first of all, whose modality will render fictional and fragile everything that follows, the entire narrative and the interpretation it brings into play. One does not testify in court and before the law with "perhaps." Furthermore, in principle, an error and an injustice are not the same thing. They are even incompatible: to do wrong by mistake is not an injustice. Here, injustice would have been a mistake, would have been done by mistake; in other words, it would have been just for him to die—perhaps. An error was made, thanks to which an injustice was committed, and we will see later how the randomness of the error committed the injustice, the injustice as error. Two orders—the ethical and, let us say, the theoretical or epistemological—intersect here, even though they remain incompatible: an error and an injustice.

My gestures are of a great violence; I know this, I confess it. It is obvious that Blanchot is publishing this, I
would not dare say at the end of his life, for he is describing to us the instance of his death from the moment he
was still this young man. But he is publishing it very late
in his life. This suspension has lasted fifty years; his letter
says so. But at a moment when his testimony and his attestation have become more testamentary than ever, like
all of his texts and all of his letters, he can always be suspected of making public this testimony in a political space
in which for some time, as we know, trials, accusations,
and even verdicts on the subject of his political past have
been multiplying. At this moment, he could be suspected
of the abuse of a fiction, that is, of a type of text whose author is not responsible, not responsible for what happens
to the narrator or the characters of the narrative, not an-
swerable before the law for the truthfulness of what he
says. One might insinuate that he is exploiting a certain ir-
responsibility of literary fiction in order to pass off, like
contraband, an allegedly real testimony, this time not fictional, coming to justify or exculpate in a historical reality
the political behavior of an author it is easy to identify
with both the narrator and the central character. In this
space, one can put forward the hypothesis that Blanchot
intends finally to mark, by means of a fiction so obviously
testimonial and autobiographical in appearance (auto-
thanatographical in truth), that he is someone the Germans wanted to shoot in a situation where he would visibly have been on the side of the Resistance fighters. One
can always call into question the purity of this testimony
and sense calculation in it. I am convinced that calculation
is not simply absent. How could it be? And in the name of
what would one want to require that it be absent, forcing
oneself thus to deprive it of any justification or explana-

tion of itself? It is therefore probably not unjustified, but
there is this calculation and we must take it into account
in our reading. Such a calculation may be extremely complex and differentiated. On the one hand, non-literary testimony is no more a proof than is testimony in the form
of a literary fiction. On the other hand, the author of the
two, always the sole witness to that of which he speaks,
may speak truly or falsely, speak truly here and falsely
there, interweave a series of interpretations, implications,
reflections, unverifiable effects around a woof or a warp
objectively recognized and beyond suspicion. We will
study the meshes of the net formed by the limits *between*
fiction and testimony, which are also *interior* each to the
other. The net's texture remains loose, unstable, perme-
able. Historical through and through, this texture is the
texture of literature and all of the passions it suffers and
sustains, to which it testifies as its truth without truth, all
of the passions with which it is swollen or which catch
themselves in it.

⁓

The following paragraph recalls a date in two short sentences, with a precision whose economy is admirable, as is
the parsimony [*principe d'épargne*] of this entire narrative.
As in the beginning of *Death Sentence*, the narrator estab-
lishes indubitable reference to an objective date (1944)
and historical situation known to all:

> The Allies had succeeded in getting a foothold on French
> soil. The Germans, already vanquished, were struggling in
> vain with useless ferocity.

This notation installs us in the indubitable landscape of
historical reality. It stamps a seal of historical realism on
everything that follows. The testimony that follows would
thus involve a reality.

In a large house (the Château, it was called), someone knocked at the door rather timidly.

It is of the utmost importance that it be a castle here, or, more precisely, what bears the name Castle, of which one says, in society: that is the Château. We evoked Dostoyevsky earlier. Kafka also always remains close to Blanchot, as we know. Visibly the young man, the other, the one who will die without dying, resides in a Castle to which *someone* wants access, at whose door "someone knocked," and "he" probably owes his life to the fact that this house bears the name *Château*. The Germans or those who, as we will see, are not Germans but Russians, will pause, will show a certain restraint before the Château, at the entrance to the residence [*demeure*]. To this name, "the Château," a name thought to incorporate into stone a name, a family, a lineage—to this name the young man will owe his respects, about which he will speak further. There would be a share of injustice here; and a sort of implicit social or social-historical critique, as will become clear later on. The name "the Château," the fact that it is an ennobled bourgeois residence [*demeure*] in some sense and as such respected by all of Europe, even postrevolutionary Europe, this will play a determining role in the story, that is, in a death without death, which was perhaps "the error of injustice."

> In a large house (the Château, it was called), someone knocked at the door rather timidly. I know that the young man . . .

One immediately sees that the "I," the narrator of the text, the inner signatory, is *the one who accompanies* the young man, we might say, thus displacing another of Blanchot's titles. He knows in advance; he has an absolute knowledge in advance of everything that happens to the young man; for he is the same, he is the one of whom the young man could say: he is the one who accompanies me. He knows in advance:

I know that the young man . . .

Everything takes place as if the narrator were shadowing this man of another age, as if he were following this young man at every instant, step by step, in order to testify to what happens or does not happen to him. As if there were, in the end, only a difference in age between them, marked by the expression "the young man." (One can imagine someone showing a photograph: look at me at this age, when I was a young man; I still remember it, the young man I will have been.)

I know that the young man came to open the door to guests [*hôtes*] who were presumably asking for help.

What the narrator knows, describes, attests to is what takes place in the young man's head: I know that this young man went to open the door because he thought, mistakenly, that those who were knocking on the door were asking for help: *hôtes*, again.

This time, a howl: "Everyone outside."

The troop forces the occupants out of their home. A classic scene and situation under the occupation by the Germans, as under any foreign occupation. The violence consists in expelling or dragging the occupants from the residence [*demeure*]:

"Everyone outside."
A Nazi lieutenant . . .

Until this point, the narrator has said "the Germans."
Now he is specific, and this precision sounds like a political stance, already an accusing objectivation that opposes
the narrator to the "Nazi" of whom he speaks:

> A Nazi lieutenant, in shamefully normal French, made the
> oldest people exit first, and then two young women.
> "Outside, outside."

"This instant, I am speaking French," the Nazi could
say, as we were saying earlier. It is a Nazi who spoke
"shamefully normal French." Shameful for whom? Shameful at least for a certain French Nazism, a Nazism whose
language is French, a Nazism that has been naturalized
French or a French that has been naturalized Nazi. Another accusation, thus, discreetly but clearly aimed at an
implicit contamination where it is essential, internal, and
fatal—the contamination through language, the complicity in language. The Nazi speaks the same language we do,
the language of my attestation itself: this is what is irreme-
diably shameful and what any attestation must begin by
avowing, becoming thus a confession, a political confession, before any determinable fault.

This time, he was howling.

An attestation that is punctuated by instantaneous
seizures, a discontinuous series of instantaneous seizures. A
little further up the page, it was "This time, a howl," which
is echoed a few lines later: "This time, he was howling."

> The young man, however, did not try to flee but advanced
> slowly, in an almost priestly manner.

The young man is recognized, if he is seen. Here, to the
furious impatience of the officer—or of anyone who still

howls today in a position of power, in good conscience, for the victim, the hostage, or the scapegoat—the young man opposes a slowness which can but exasperate the Nazi in whatever language he is speaking. We must take this slowness into account.

> The lieutenant shook him, showed him the casings, bullets; there had obviously been fighting; the soil was a war soil.

Although the narrative remains very elliptical, one takes it that if the "Nazis" have invaded, it is because the lieutenant suspects Resistance fighters in the area. He wants to take hostages, no doubt, to shoot Resistance fighters or their accomplices. By showing the young man the bullets and casings, the lieutenant accuses him of belonging to the Resistance, or of being the enemy. He is an enemy; he is treated as an enemy, as an enemy of the Nazis. This is essential to the testimonial message that passes into the blood of reality through the epidermis of fiction.

> The lieutenant choked in a bizarre language. . . .

Earlier the Nazi spoke "shamefully normal French." Any Nazi, whatever his nationality, can speak shamefully normal French. He can speak whatever language from whatever continent. Here, he is choking. Earlier he was howling; now, he is choking "in a bizarre language," as if he were changing languages or rediscovering the truth of his own, the Nazi language which is not a language.

> And putting the casings, the bullets, a grenade under the nose of the man already less young (one ages quickly), he distinctly shouted . . .

The munitions exposed are thus exhibits, evidence in a trial, clues that can dispense with testimony. The nota-

tion in parentheses, "(one ages quickly)," marks a sort of
parenthesis of time that recalls the parenthesis: namely,
that times passes without passing, like a parenthesis, in
parentheses, the measure of time remaining here an absolutely heterogeneous measure. The time that separates
the moment that a Nazi shoves casings in one's face from
the moment he threatens one with death is both much
shorter and much longer: it is an entire lifetime in an instant, an eternity. A change of age. What will happen will
have opened another time. Absolute anachrony of a time
out of joint. The notations concerning age thus have a
great importance. The narrative, we will remember, begins with "a man still young," here "already less young
(one ages quickly)," whereas, according to the objective
and realistic chronology of the narrative, barely a few
seconds have elapsed. These two times, that of objectivity and that of phantasm or fictional simulacrum, which
is also that of testimonial experience, remain absolutely
incommensurable:

> The lieutenant . . . distinctly shouted: "This is what you
> have come to."

Accusation and trial. What becomes of the witness, or
rather the narrator, who is here the witness *for* the witness?
No one testifies for the witness, says Celan. Here the narrator testifies for the witness, that is, for the young man.
The witness *for* the witness, the narrator, testifies first *for*
an accused. The latter will be condemned to death, but
first he is an accused. The narrator must testify to a fun-
damental accusation, already to a verdict that leads to
death. "This is what you have come to."

> The Nazi placed his men in a row in order to hit, according
> to the rules, the human target.

This is what is called a "firing squad." The men are there, ready with their guns, and it will be a question of shooting.

> The young man said, "At least have my family go inside." So it was: the aunt (ninety-four years old); his mother, younger; his sister and sister-in-law; a long, slow procession, silent, as if everything had already been done.

There are no men around him, only women. He is the only man and thus the last man, this man already less young. *The Last Man* is not only the title of another of Blanchot's books. The eschatology of the last man is marked in the phrase that states in the mode of fiction ("as if") that the end has already taken place before the end: "as if everything had already been done." Death has already taken place, however unexperienced its experience may remain in the absolute acceleration of a time infinitely contracted into the point of an instant. The screenplay is so clear, and it describes the action so explicitly in two lines, that the program is exhausted in advance. We know everything with an absolute knowledge. Everything, all of it, has already happened because we know what is going to happen. We know the screenplay; we know what is going to happen. It is over; it is already over from the instant of the credits. It begins with the end; as in *The Madness of the Day*, it begins with the end. We know it happened. "As if everything were already done," it already happened. The end of time.

What will happen now will thus sink into what was done, as it were backward, into what had already arrived, into what has already arrived, that is to say, death. The women who leave know, as does the young man, as does the last man and his shadow, witness to a witness, that death has already arrived, because it is inescapable. One is not resuscitated from this experience of inescapable death, even if one survives it. One can only survive it without surviving it. If one wanted to speak here of resurrection through the experience of a Christlike passion (the Germans would be the Romans, this time), there would be no Christology, no speculative Good Friday, no truth of religion in the absolute knowledge of Hegel, whose spectral shadow will not be long in passing. But all of this—the Passion, the Resurrection, absolute Knowledge—is mimicked, repeated, and displaced. Already in the life without life of this *survivance*, henceforth, as it were, fictional, all knowledge will tremble, and with it all testimonial statement in the form of knowledge: "I know—do I know it—," without question marks. The paragraph that begins thus tells of the knowledge and the indecision regarding knowledge that the narrator-witness continues to invoke on the subject of the other, the old young man, the last man that he is, the last man by name, the last to remain [*demeurer*] from the Château:

> I know—do I know it—that the one at whom the Germans were already aiming, awaiting but the final order, experienced then a feeling of extraordinary lightness, a sort of beatitude (nothing happy, however)—sovereign elation? The encounter of death with death?

It is not enough to pay careful attention to the letter and the economy of these words. For the eye and the breath, first, one must give way in silence to the punctuation: the absence of question marks after "I know—do I know—," followed by multiple question marks where the verb remains omitted ("sovereign elation? The encounter of death with death?"), and in both cases a principle of uncertainty, a *perhaps* that modalizes, "epochalizes," and suspends all assertions of the narrator-witness. He never affirms anything, never commits himself to any assertion. One should also note the substitution of "beatitude" for "happiness" in a sort of negative approach of what remains to be said, as sovereignty itself, perhaps. The question marks suspend everything in an *epokhē* of judgment such as I underlined at the beginning of the narrative on the subject of the "perhaps." The sovereignty of "sovereign beatitude" *perhaps* prevails, in death itself, over the mastery of power that brings death, over the mastery of the Nazi occupier.

Many other of Blanchot's texts, in particular the double "A Primitive Scene," name a furtive moment, a scene where hardly anything at all is recounted, where perhaps nothing arrives. A child, perhaps the same as this "young man," experiences through tears, following something that resembles an unspoken trauma, a feeling of lightness or beatitude. "Sovereign elation?" Another question: "The encounter of death with death?" With a question mark, this last question may appear tautological, redundant, or hollow, unless it is saying the essential, namely, death itself, for once, at the tip of the instant of imminence, at gun point, *at the moment when* and *from the moment that* death was going to arrive—because he has not been shot yet. Perhaps it is the encounter of death, which is only ever an imminence, only ever an instance, only ever a suspension, an anticipation, the encounter of death as anticipation with death itself, with a death that has already arrived according to the inescapable: an encounter between what is going to arrive and what has already arrived. Between what is on the point of arriving and what has just arrived, between what is going to come [*va venir*] and what just finished coming [*vient de venir*], between what goes and comes. But as the same. Both virtual and real, real as virtual. What has arrived has arrived insofar as it

announces itself as what must inescapably arrive. Death
has just come from the instant it is going to come. It has
come to pass insofar as it comes; it has come as soon as it
is going to come. *It has just finished coming.* Death encounters itself. The moment death encounters *itself,* going
to the encounter with itself, at this moment both inescapable and improbable, the arrival of death at itself, this
arrival of a death that never arrives and never happens to
me—at this instant lightness, elation, beatitude remain
the only affects that can take measure of this event as "an
unexperienced experience." What can an unexperienced
feeling signify? How would one experience it? Dying will
finally become possible—as prohibition. All living beings
have an impossible relation to death; at the instant death,
the impossible, will become possible as impossible. This is
what, by defying analysis, also gives lightness and sovereign elation:

> In his place [in the place of the young man], I will not try to
> analyze.

In the future, *thus now,* I will not try to analyze in the
place of the young man whom I could no longer replace
today even if he were the same as me. The self itself. Is
there a witness who would dare say this? And yet is there a
witness who must not say this, in all conscience, namely:
"At the moment of my attestation I am no longer the same
as the witness who lived that and who remains irreplaceable"? The signature of the narrator is thus dated. This is
the difference both null and uncrossable, real and fictional,
actual and virtual, between the one who says "I" and the
"I" of the young man of whom he speaks and who is himself, whom he still remembers according to the synthesis of
which we spoke earlier. The one who says and undersigns
"I" today, now, cannot replace the other; he can no longer,

therefore, replace himself, that is, the young man he has been. He can no longer replace him, substitute himself for him, a condition that is nonetheless stipulated for any normal and non-fictional testimony. He can no longer relive what has been lived. And thus, in a certain way, he no longer knows, he has a memory of what he no longer knows ("I know—do I know it—," do I know; do I know what I know, me, I, me the I . . .). In other words, he testifies *for* a witness, in a different sense this time, *in the place* of the witness he cannot be *for* this other witness that the young man was, and who is yet himself. The young man was a witness to the death that came at him [*venait sur lui*]. The witness to this witness, who is the same, fifty years later, cannot replace the witness for whom he testifies. Consequently, he cannot analyze what he himself felt, this other himself, at that moment. An odd experience, but at the same time very banal. Every one of us can say at every instant: really, I don't remember what I felt; I can't describe what I felt at that moment; it's impossible, and I can't analyze it in any case. What was me is no longer me, the *ego cogito*, the "I think that accompanies all of my representations" is but an empty form in which I do not recognize anything; this universal "I" was not me, the me that is speaking to you; I can no longer (and do not ask me to, it would be violence) answer for what this other me— more other than any other—did, or even thought or felt because of the troubling vertiginousness that calls into the chasm of that instant and especially because what separates the two egological identities is nothing less than death itself, that is to say, everything, an infinite world. The two die but he is dead, I survive, he survived, I am dead. If both die, which one remains to survive to say it?

He was perhaps suddenly invincible.

Totally exposed, vulnerable, disarmed, offered unto death, a being for death, the young man seems to represent the very opposite of invincibility, of course. But "perhaps"! ("perhaps . . . invincible"). And yet the inexorability of what was coming at him, of what was imminent, but which had thus already arrived, "perhaps" made him invincible. Invincible because totally vanquished, totally exposed, totally lost.

Dead—immortal.

The syntax of this sentence without sentence, of this death without sentence of which Blanchot also speaks elsewhere, sums up everything in a single stroke. No verb. A hyphen, a line of union and separation, a disjunctive link wordlessly marks the place of all logical modalities: dead *and yet* immortal, dead *because* immortal, dead *insofar as* immortal (an immortal does not live), immortal *from the moment that* and *insofar as* dead, *although* and *for as long as* dead; for once dead one no longer dies and, according to all possible modes, one has become immortal, thus accustoming oneself to—nothing. He is already dead, since there has been a verdict, but an immortal is someone who is dead. When one is dead, it does not happen twice, there are not two deaths even if two die. Consequently, only someone who is dead is immortal—in other words, the immortals are dead. What happens to him is immortality, with death and as death, at the same instant. Not a Platonic or Christian immortality in the moment of death or of the Passion when the soul finally gathers together as it leaves the body, having already been at work there in philosophy according to the *ēpimeleia tou thanatou* of a pre-Christian *Phaedo*. No, it is in death that immortality yields to an "unexperienced experience," in the instant of death, when death arrives, where one is *not*

yet dead in order to be *already* dead, at the same instant.
At the same instant, but the tip of the instant is divided
here: I am not dead *and* I am dead. At that instant, I am
immortal because I am dead: death can no longer happen
to me. It is prohibited. Hence an experience of immortality—the happiness of nearly being shot to death, said the
letter, the letter which spoke of "happiness" where the
published text refuses the word, at least refuses it at this
moment, for the word "happiness" will appear in an instant, which allows for this terrible murmur also to become a testimony to happiness.

Dead—immortal. Perhaps ecstasy.

A vocabulary with mystical resonances is elicited by the
secret and by the singularity of an unexperienced experience: going outside of oneself, beatitude, elation, lightness,
ecstasy. An ecstatic wrenching from common temporal existence, an immense orgiastic jouissance—to translate this
ecstatic beatitude into a language which is not Blanchot's.
It is jouissance and one can play at retranslating what we
are told here into all the experiences of sensuous pleasure
that have extraordinary ecstasy, invincibility, lightness to of-
fer. It is jouissance insofar as it does not go without death:
"Perhaps ecstasy," says the witness to himself as another.
    Declaring that he will not try to analyze in the place of
the young man, he nonetheless proposes descriptive
words and schemas: "perhaps," "rather"—"He was *perhaps*
suddenly invincible"—"*Perhaps* ecstasy." I underline the
"perhaps," the modality of his entire discourse; a little earlier, when he writes: "I know—do I know it—" without
question mark, the "do I know it—" means "perhaps"—
and unleashes a trembling in the assertion, in the certainty, a trembling that leaves its mark and its essential
modality on the entire discourse of the possible *perhaps.*

That of the thinkers of the future, said Nietzsche. Nothing is certain in this testimony, nothing is described, nothing is observable: everything only *may be*. A random virtuality that is less than ever opposed to the actuality of the act or presence.

> Rather the feeling of compassion for suffering humanity, the happiness of not being immortal or eternal.

This "neither immortal nor eternal" might resemble the reversal of the earlier, sentenceless ellipsis: "dead—immortal." But this is not the case at all. The "dead—immortal" did not in the least signify eternity. The immortality of death is anything save the eternity of the present. The abidance [*demeurance*] that we will discuss does not *remain* like the permanence of an eternity. It is time itself. This non-philosophical and non-religious experience of immortality *as death* gives without rupturing solitude, in the ecstasy itself: it gives compassion for all mortals, for all humans who suffer; and the happiness, this time, of not being immortal—or eternal. At this instant there can be elation, lightness in the immortality of death, happiness in compassion, a sharing of finitude, a friendship with finite beings, in the happiness of not being immortal—or eternal.

> Henceforth, he was bound to death by a surreptitious friendship.

The compassion for suffering humanity, thus for a passion of death, is a bond without bond, the disjointing, the disadjusting of a social bond that binds only, in truth, to death and on condition of death: on condition of mortal being.

∼

Blanchot's *Friendship*—not only the book that bears this title and not only the friendship he speaks of in this book, and not only for Bataille—is here allied with a *passion of death*, as to its element and its condition. A friendship for death. Friendship assumes the experience of death; it is a matter of the friendship with death. He comes to love this death. There is an alliance—"bound to death," he says— a contract, a familiarity, a collusion with death and for always. The crypt of a secret friendship, unpublishable, unavowable, "surreptitious." Every sentence of this text gives us, let us not say a key, but at least a prescription for reading Blanchot's entire work, as if the "unexperienced experience" of the event he was recounting had, in advance, given its law, its grammar and its destiny to everything he has since written.

At that instant . . .

So begins the following paragraph.

This is why we had to begin with the instant today. "At that instant" the scene will turn or topple over into the revolution of a single instant. There has already been an instant in which death happened to him. Everything was preprogrammed; it was inevitable and fatal, it has thus already arrived—death. And yet, in this very "it has arrived," *another instant* will, in some sense, cause the world, existence, and ecstasy itself to be overturned.

To this instant he will testify.

At that instant, an abrupt return to the world . . .

Death had already taken place. It had arrived from the moment the young man began to wait for "the final order," the "Fire" of the lieutenant. He had thus left the world, dying before dying, not for another world, but for a non-world beyond life, not for a transcendent beyond or the beyond that religions and metaphysics tell us about, but for a here-below without world, a beyond here-below, a without-world from which he who is already dead already returns, like a ghost, the moment gunfire suddenly explodes in the vicinity. Another "fire," a counterfire.

> At that instant, an abrupt return to the world, the considerable noise of a nearby battle exploded. Comrades from the maquis wanted to bring help to one they knew to be in danger.

Here things seem very clear and the reality of the referent appears to be named deliberately beyond the perforated veil, the net or mesh of fiction. Literature serves as real testimony. Literature pretends, through an excess of fiction—others would say lie—to pass itself off as a real and responsible testimony about a historical reality—without, however, signing this testimony because it is literature and the narrator is not the author of an autobiography. We are clearly given to understand that the Resistance fighters, the friends of the young man, the accomplices of the fictional character, are also the allies of the narrator, who is "the same" as the character, the "young man," and by contagion the allies of Maurice Blanchot, whom one also suspects of being the same as the narrator, who is none other than the "young man," the friend of the "comrades from the maquis." Conclusion, *Dichtung und Wahrheit*, the Resistance fighters, the "comrades from the maquis," who were the friends of the young man, are the allies and friends of the narrator, who in truth is none other than Maurice Blanchot. A way of saying to all the prosecutors of the world and elsewhere, of this continent and the other continents, that the people of the maquis were comrades and *his* comrades. The author could count himself among the Resistance fighters. He was in the war against the Nazis as he was against the genocidal anti-Semites.

Comrades from the maquis wanted to bring help to one they knew to be in danger.

In other words—let us always say "in other words," for it is always a matter here of saying *otherwise said* and a certain slippage of the *that is to say*—"bring help," in other words, "help" and salvation of me, of me, *that is to say*, of the young man, of the young man, *that is to say*, of the narrator, the first and last witness, the intimate witness of the young man, of the narrator witness, *that is to say*, of the author who slips in behind the *I* of the narrator. The slippage of these three metonymic "*that is to say*'s," the play of these three *I*'s, is a passion of literature as passion of death and compassion among these three instances (author, narrator, character); it is the passion in literature, what the perverse limit between *Dichtung und Wahrheit* suffers, endures, tolerates, and cultivates. The *that is to say* never signs. No one will dare assume the right, because no one will ever have it, to say that these three *I*'s are the same; no one will ever answer for this identity of compassion. It is a fiction of testimony more than a testimony in which the witness swears to tell the truth, the whole truth, and nothing but the truth. But allow me, for lack of time, to say this too quickly: without the *possibility* of this fiction, without the spectral virtuality of this simulacrum and as a result of this lie or this fragmentation of the true, no truthful testimony would be possible. Consequently, the possibility of literary fiction haunts so-called truthful, responsible, serious, real testimony as its proper possibility. This haunting is perhaps the passion itself, the passionate place of literary writing, as the project to say everything—and wherever it is auto-biographical, that is to say, everywhere, and everywhere autobio-thanatographical.

The lieutenant moved away [*s'éloigna*] to assess the situation.

The scene of imminence becomes clear in the discreet series of these *instantaneous seizures*, everything is ready: the firing squad is ready to fire, waiting, like the young man, for "the final order"; the lieutenant is ready to give it, this order. Everything is *in order*, the order of absolute imminence, when suddenly, from one instant to the next, an absolute interruption of absolute imminence, the lieutenant hears a noise in the distance, he moves away for an instant. *He does not leave, he moves away.* The movement away, the "moving away" is one of the most discreetly effective and recurrent words of the narrative; we will return to this more than once. No one leaves or escapes, especially not the young man, the last man, but everyone *moves away.*

> The Germans stayed in order . . .

In other words, the soldiers remain "in order" waiting for the "final order" (the same word, "order" in two absolutely different senses). The second-class soldiers, immobile, remain ready to fire while the lieutenant takes a few steps to see what is happening, because of the detonations that, at that instant, come to disturb the scenario, to interrupt the fatal progress of the execution. As if the sudden interruption of an order were nothing less than the interruption of time itself. Revolution. The testimony testifies to nothing less than the instant of an interruption of time and history, a second of interruption in which fiction and testimony find their common resource.

> The Germans stayed in order, prepared to *remain* [demeurer] thus in an immobility that arrested time. [My emphasis]

Such an instant does not follow in the temporal sequence of instants; this instant is another eternity, the stance or station of another present. Suddenly, the pro-

gram of execution is fixed, prepared to *remain* [demeurer]
for eternity. The soldiers are there, they will not move so
long as they do not receive the order to do something else.
This instantaneous seizure resembles a painting (it is executed like an execution by Goya or Manet, *May Third,
1808* (1814) or the *Execution of Maximilian* (1867–69), two
more events with obliquely Napoleonic references).
Freeze-frame in the unfolding of a film in a movie camera:
the soldiers are there, they no longer move, neither does
the young man, an eternal instant, another eternal instant.

> Then one of them approached and said in a firm voice,
> "We're not Germans, Russians," and, with a sort of laugh,
> "Vlassov army," and made a sign for him to disappear.

In other words, one soldier moves, a single one among
them. Everything will depend on this unique initiative,
singular and solitary, in truth unique and unexpected on
the part of a soldier: an original who separates himself
from the group to which he belongs. Everything will
hinge on this separation, which intensifies the disparity in
nationality. The Vlassov army is another ineffaceable referent anchoring literature to a confirmed historical reality;
it was a Russian army that put itself in the service of the
Nazis. Vlassov was a Russian general who—to summarize
in a word the very complex process in its premises and final evolution—went over to the enemy, to the German
side, with his army. He figures as a sort of collaborator,
but the analogy is superficial. Some of the soldiers who
held the young man, his witness, and the author at gun-
point were thus Russian soldiers and not German soldiers.
Salvation came from the Russians and not the Nazis. The
allusion to Dostoyevsky is even more tempting: he also escaped execution at the last instant through what was a
pardon, the clemency [*grâce*] of an emperor who thought

that he could possess literature by playing with the life of a great writer. It is by the Russians that the French writer was almost executed and thanks to whom miraculously but without grace [*grâce*] he escapes death.

(I intentionally say "miraculously" to suggest something I will not have the time to develop further, namely, that any testimony testifies in essence to the miraculous and the extraordinary from the moment it must, by definition, appeal to an act of faith beyond any proof. When one testifies, even on the subject of the most ordinary and the most "normal" event, one asks the other to believe one at one's word as if it were a matter of a miracle. Where it shares its condition with literary fiction, testimoniality belongs *a priori* to the order of the miraculous. This is why reflection on testimony has always historically privileged the example of miracles. The miracle is the essential line of union between testimony and fiction. And the passion we are discussing goes hand in hand with the miraculous, the fantastic, the phantasmatic, the spectral, vision, apparition, the touch of the untouchable, the experience of the extraordinary, history without nature, the anomalous. This is also why it is a canonical passion, canonizable, in the European-Christian-Roman sense.)

Thus an interruption of dying is at issue, a salvation by the Resistance and by a Russian. An act of the French Resistance has interrupted the process of execution and the Resistance has been taken over by a Russian who, in abnormal and borrowed French, has betrayed his commander and betrayed the betrayal of Vlassov.

> "We're not Germans, Russians," and, with a sort of laugh, "Vlassov army," and made a sign for him to disappear.

The question of language is certainly important. The "German" lieutenant is a "Nazi" who apparently "spoke

shamefully normal French," but one of the soldiers, who is
Russian and not German, speaks normal French: "'We're
not Germans, Russians.'"

⁓

In other words, the Russian betrays the German to save
"Blanchot" (you know why I am putting this proper noun
in quotation marks, henceforth). He saves "Blanchot," he
assures his salvation by telling him, in short, "Go, save
yourself." The passion of this instant of my death is a
story of salvation, a passion as salvation, but of a salvation
that has come from someone who salutes the other and
saves him by saying, "Save yourself." Without apparent
Christian soteriology.

Naturally, "Blanchot" does not run off; this would be
unworthy. It is not said that he took to his heels at top
speed, out of fear, but that he moved away ("I think he
moved away"), no doubt with the same slowness, "almost
priestly," as the young man at the beginning of the narrative shortly before, of whom it was already said, let us remember—and the art of composition is as always admirable—that he did not flee ("The young man . . . did
not try to flee but advanced slowly, in an almost priestly
manner"). Now again he saves himself [*se sauve*] without
fleeing, or rather, he assures his salvation without running
away [without saving himself: *sans se sauver*]. But one already knows that this very salvation will not have saved
him from death, which will already have taken place in
any event. It is a salvation without salvation. And twice
more, for the third time at least, the vocabulary of distance insists at very close intervals: "he moved away"
. . . in the direction of "a distant forest":

> I think he moved away, still with the feeling of lightness, un-
> til he found himself in a distant forest, named the "Bois des

bruyères," where he remained [*demeura*] sheltered by trees he knew well.

"He *remained* [demeura] sheltered. . . ." If we had the time, we might have been able and we would have had to follow the specifically *lingering* insistence of the abode and the abiding [*l'insistance proprement* demeurante *de la demeure et du demeurer*] in *The Instant of My Death*. And the word "abode, abiding [*demeure, demeurer*]" often returns in the text, which thus remains [*demeure*] untranslatable (someone who is present here has had a firsthand experience of this),[15] where the signifying form *demeure* plays on what dies, with the "unexperienced experience" of the one who dies, where two die, do not die, or remain [*demeurent*] or un-die [*dé-meurent*] in the moment in which they die, but also with what stays on and maintains itself through time in an abode [*demeure*], a house, the rooms, and a Château whose premises form the constant foyer of the descriptions and references. As if the abode [*demeure*]—its abidance [*sa demeurance*]—were the true central character, at the same time being the scene, the place, and the taking place of the narrative. Everything that happens, in the instant, happens because of and in the proximity of the Château; everything happens without happening to the Château, to the abode [*la demeure*] in which the one who was "prevented from dying by death itself" resides [*demeure*]: "In a large house (the Château, it was called)."

The abiding of the abode [*le demeurer de la demeure*] is specifically named at least five times. Before listing them, I will call to mind, among all of those that are important to us here, several of the semantic features of this rare word, enigmatic and strictly untranslatable. It is a word with a Latin root, again, which, through Provençal, Span-

ish (*demorar*), or Italian (*demorari*), leads one back to the
Latin *demorari, de* and *mourari*, which signifies *to wait*
and *to delay*. There is always the idea of a wait, a con-
tretemps, a delay, or a reprieve in a *demeure* as there is in a
moratorium. In great-French-literature, the *demeure* as the
waiting or the appeal [*instance*] was made to rhyme with
the word *meurt*. Corneille: "Oui, sans plus de demeure,
Pour l'intérêt des dieux je consens qu'elle meure [Yes,
without further delay, In the interest of the Gods I con-
sent to her death]." *Etre en demeure* is to be late, and *met-
tre en demeure*, in juridical language, is to summon someone to fulfill an obligation within an allotted time. The
extension to a home, a lodging, a residence, a house first
stems from the time given for the occupation of a space
and goes as far as the "final resting place [*dernière demeure*]" where the dead reside. There would be no end to
the mortuary and moratory avenues of this vocabulary
that we could visit. Old French also had this word that I
have already used, in an approximate way, I think: *la demeurance*, which was also written—more strikingly and
very appropriately for our text, *la demourance*.

Here, then, are the five reminders of such a *demourance*
in *The Instant of My Death*. Each time the grammatical
form is different, hence each occurrence is unique, without
the least weakness of distracted repetition (*demeurer, demeura, demeure* [the noun], *demeure* [the verb], *demeurait*).

1. "The Germans stayed in order, prepared to *remain*
[demeurer] thus in an immobility that arrested time."

2. Lower, on the same page: "he found himself in a distant forest, named the 'Bois des bruyères,' where he *remained* [demeura] sheltered by trees he knew well."

3. Further, the home [*la demeure*] is none other than
Hegel's, and we are not through with this analogy or this
contrast: "Lie and truth: for as Hegel wrote to another

friend, the French pillaged and ransacked his *home* [*sa* de-meure]." We will return to this, and to this "Lie and truth" that resonates like an echo of the contemporary *Dichtung und Wahrheit* of someone who also had dealings with Napoleon.

4. The last sentence of the narrative, which brings together the essential, describes "all that remains [*demeure*]"; and "all that remains" is the very death of the one who dies: "All that *remains* is the feeling of lightness, which is death itself or, to put it more precisely, the instant of my death henceforth always in abeyance."

5. This last sentence repeats another sentence a little further up, which begins in an even more striking way with the verb *demeurait*, placed at the head and origin of the statement in order to characterize what is called by the same words and thus gives the most abiding [*demeurante*] note, the *demourance* of the entire narrative, affecting it with its most essential affect, "the feeling of lightness":

> There *remained* however [Demeurait *cependant*], at the moment when the shooting was no longer but to come, the feeling of lightness that I would not know how to translate. . . .

This *demeurait* is in keeping with the sense of *demeurance*, namely, as the same sentence says, of being "to come."

∼

Let us go back a little further:

> In the dense forest, suddenly, after how much time, he rediscovered a sense of the real.

Chronological notations, indications of time abound. "Blanchot" or the narrator is constantly underlining the duration, the non-duration, the impossibility of measuring the duration or the *demourance*. This chronometry re-

mains paradoxical and removed from objective knowledge: "after how much time" is another question without
question mark—he does not know "after how much time,
he rediscovered a sense of the real." And thus, perhaps, if
he ever rediscovered it.

A time of return. There is a return to the world when
the shooting explodes. In this return to the world, he
moves away without running away. Only once he has escaped without escaping [*s'est sauvé sans se sauver*] does he
return to the real. This implies that until this instant, in
this unbelievable scenario, he had, in some sense, left the
real. All of this was not real in a certain manner—to par-
ody by inversion the sentence from *The Madness of the
Day*. Here "he rediscovered a sense of the real." Both fictional and real, this testimony could not put itself forward
as fiction if it did not lay claim to reality.

> Everywhere fires, a continuous succession of fires; all the farms
> were burning. *A little later*, he learned that three young men,
> sons of farmers—truly strangers to all combat, whose only
> fault was their youth—had been slaughtered. [My emphasis]

Not only is it a matter of a chronometry without measure, but it is also a question of the impossible measure of
time according to age and generation; whence the quick ag-
ing of those who are young ("three young men . . . whose
only fault was their youth"). Something he "learned" "a little later."

> Even the bloated horses, on the road, in the fields, *attested* to
> a war that had gone on. [My emphasis]

The verb "attested," which I underline, is the only word
that explicitly signals the testimonial dimension of the
narrative. It is employed, furthermore, in a diverted and
derivative sense: a thing or an animal, *a fortiori*, a body

could never attest to anything, even if it does attest, in the loose sense of being a clue or evidence. In the humanist logic of what we call testimony in our European culture, a horse does not testify. Nor does a body. The death of a horse does not testify to the fact that there has been war unless one is using the word *attest* in a rather vague sense, in the sense of an exhibit, of a document or an archive.

> Even the bloated horses, on the road, in the fields, attested to a war that had gone on.

The war "had gone on." This new chronometric notation again plays on the paradox. It is first, in appearance, commensurate this time with the hostilities whose sequence is still unfinished, although the state of war *remains* [demeure]: the bodies of the horses are bloated because they have long since been abandoned. But the following question repeats the "how much time" on the same page; it seems to concern—with a question mark this time—the time of the present scene: "In reality, how much time had elapsed?" Again, above on the same page, the witness in effect asked: "after how much time," and here, at the bottom of the page, "how much time had elapsed?" A disturbance in the measure of time and a paradoxy of these instants, which are so many heterogeneous times. Neither synchrony nor diachrony, an anachrony of all instants. *Demourance* as anachrony. There is not a single time, and since there is not a single time, since one instant has no common measure with any other because of death, by reason of death interposed, in the interruption by reason of death, so to speak, because of the cause of the death there can be no chronology or chronometry. One cannot, even when one has recovered a sense of the real, measure time. And thus the question returns, how many times: how much time? how much time? how much time?

What Blanchot's text attests to, what it wants to testify to, is, basically, that for the last fifty years, in spite of
the anniversary he tells me about, July 20, 1994, time has
not been measurable. Blanchot has remained the one
who remained back there, undying [*demourant*] in the
same *restance*—who died that day, who died without dying, who escaped without escaping [*qui a été sauvé sans
se sauver*]; but for how much time? Fifty years? Fifty
thousand years? No time. The time of *demourance* is
incommensurable.

> When the lieutenant returned and became aware the young
> chatelaine had disappeared, why did anger, rage, not prompt
> him to burn down the Château (immobile and majestic)?
> Because it was the Château.

From the beginning of the text, we are reminded that
this residence [*demeure*] is called "the Château," not only
on account of the monumental nobility of the notation, of
the reference to all castles in the world, especially Kafka's
castle, but also because this castle is an authority [*instance*], a socio-political figure that will play a role in the
unfolding and in the macro-historical, ideological-politi-
cal and socio-juridical interpretation of the testimonial
thing. Several sentences bring together everything that
this castle or this reference to the castle mobilizes in terms
of historical memory, coincidences, crossings, anniver-
saries, hypermnesic superimpositions. This Château becomes a palimpsest for the entire history of Europe. This
residence [*demeure*] harbors the essential archive of
modernity. In the genial and genealogical economy of an
elliptical narrative that occupies no more space than a
missive, in the absolute brevity of an event that did not arrive, so to speak, in what arrived without arriving, the entire memory of European modernity comes to be meton-

ymized. There is here the genius of the witness who reminds us that the testimonial act is poetic or it is not, from the moment it must invent its language and form itself in an incommensurable performative.

> On the facade was inscribed, like an indestructible reminder, the date 1807.

An unflagging interest in the date, the anniversary, the return takes hold of the witness at this point. As at the beginning of the letter outside literature that I can attest to having received a year ago. "July 20. Fifty years ago, I knew the happiness of nearly being shot to death."

> . . . like an indestructible reminder, the date 1807. Was he cultivated enough [the lieutenant] to know this was the famous year of Jena,[16] when Napoleon, on his small gray horse, passed under the windows of Hegel, who recognized in him the "spirit of the world," as he wrote to a friend? Lie and truth: as Hegel wrote to another friend . . . [*There is always more than one truth because there are several friends. Hegel had more than one friend, and he did not testify to the same thing before each of them. They all spoke German, the same language, but, perhaps, without lying, Hegel told this to one and that to the other about the historical truth of what was happening; and the difference is not nothing, as you will see.*] Lie and truth, for, as Hegel wrote to another friend, the French pillaged and ransacked his *home* [*sa* demeure]. [My emphasis]

Just and unjust return of things between France and her neighbors: what happened to the Hegel residence [*demeure*] is, in short, a little like what happened, much later, in the Château, to "Blanchot's" residence [*demeure*]. Except what the French did was worse, in not respecting the home [*demeure*] of the thinker of the end of history and absolute knowledge. If we had to save time, save on time or beat time to it, we would insert here, in a big book, an immense chapter on Hegel and Blanchot via Mallarmé and a few others.

Here, the Château was spared—it might have been pillaged—but the scene was much the same. The Germans—or their German Russians, the Nazi Russians of Vlassov—had come to do, let us not forget, something like what the French of the French Revolution had gone to do in Germany, in the days following the French Revolution and under the pretext of exporting the revolution to Europe:

> . . . the French pillaged and ransacked his home [*demeure*]. But Hegel knew how to distinguish the empirical and the essential.

There are friends to whom one abandons the empirical and friends to whom one confides the essential. Friendship is this as well.[17] If anyone insists on this distinction, it is Hegel. We have famous examples of some of his replies on the subject. When he did not want to hear something discussed, something he wanted to be rid of—for example, a natural child—he said that it was an empirical accident.

> In that year 1944, the Nazi lieutenant had for the Château a respect or consideration that the farms did not arouse. Everything was searched, however. Some money was taken [thus they pillaged, these Germans or these Russians—as the French pillaged in 1806]; in a separate room, "the high chamber."

"[T]he high chamber" is contained within quotation marks. The witness-author, the witness of the witness-narrator who knows everything, who has an absolute knowledge of what he speaks of, he knows in particular that there was in the residence [*demeure*] a room called the "high chamber." It was probably his own room, he resided [*demeurait*] there, he wrote there, since:

> . . . the lieutenant found papers and a sort of thick manuscript—which perhaps contained war plans.

Between "manuscript" and "which," the dash indicates a change of person. The young man or the witness of the young man knows that this manuscript had nothing to do with war plans. Yet the lieutenant takes them because he thinks that they are war plans. They were probably written work of Blanchot's—but the lieutenant takes them, saying to himself: perhaps these are war documents, a war plan. Thus "which perhaps contained war plans" is the hypothesis formed by the lieutenant. The witness of the witness has passed surreptitiously into the head of the lieutenant and conjectures about a hypothesis that may have been formed there.

> Finally he left. Everything was burning, except the Château. The Seigneurs had been spared.

All of this forms an apocalyptic scene of Last Judgment. This narrative-testimony is also a complaint and an accusation. Blanchot, or at least the narrator, is in some sense complaining about, bringing an accusation—injustice, error and injustice—against his having been saved and his residence's having been saved for an impure, unavowable, socially suspect reason, shameful thus for a reason that calls all the more for an urgent confession; and this narrative of self-justification is also, inversely, the confession of the unavowable. But through the self-justification, through the confession, another accusation, another complaint can be heard at the same time: that everything was saved *except the manuscript*. We will return to this loss of a manuscript, but, as we noted a moment ago, let us also recall Hegel's worry over his manuscript in the middle of the Napoleonic invasion.

Everything was saved, without his ever having saved himself, because he was taken for a Seigneur. The residence [*demeure*] was saved because it was taken for a Castle that belonged to the seigniorial race. When one knows what *Seigneur* signified at that moment in the Nazi code, this complaint or this accusation can only be inspired by a registered anti-Nazism. "The Seigneurs had been spared," but not the farms or the farmers. A feudal scene. The farms are burned; the young farmers, who had nothing to do with the whole thing, have been executed. But one respects the Seigneur or the residence [*demeure*] of the Seigneur.

> No doubt what then began for the young man was the torment of injustice.

The initial allusion to injustice is here made clear, at least in part. Second occurrence of the word "injustice." *The Instant of My Death* is also a meditation on justice— "and perhaps the error of injustice." It may also be a thesis on the error that is *perhaps* found at the root of all injustice. This might serve, incidentally—insofar as no one is voluntarily unjust but only unjust due to error—to exculpate or attenuate any breach of justice, including, although not only, any breach of the law: for example, in testimony.

Through his own personal salvation, the saving of his life, but also the saving of his home [*demeure*], a young man experiences social and political injustice, a revolutionary experience. This torment has never ceased, just as the suffering born of this death which was not one has never ceased. Which was not even one, but several, in incalculable number.

> No more ecstasy; the feeling that he was only living because,
> even in the eyes of the Russians, he belonged to a noble class.

"Even in the eyes of the Russians," not only for the
Nazis, for the Germans, but for these Russians, whom one
can associate, at least vaguely, with the Revolution: even
for them, a castle is invulnerable. This abode [*demeure*]
must be "respected" or protected. He who without dying
dies abidingly [*à demeure*] will have benefited from an injustice, he and his home, his home, that is to say, his family. He has benefited from an injustice, and he will not
cease to suffer from this privilege. This torment will be the
torment of an entire life, life as the torment of an injustice,
as an *inexpiable* fault, inexpiable because it was his without
being his. Everything happens as if he had to attempt the
impossible redemption of a sin or a temptation which was
also that of others, yes, the suffering of a sort of Passion. A
non-redeeming passion, a passion that would not only suffer for salvation, forgiveness, or redemption, but first a passion as transgression of a prohibition. *The Step Not Beyond*
says it in other words, in a sentence that could attend to
our encounter: "Transgression transgresses out of passion,
patience, passivity." Transgression is thus not a decision,
certainly not a decision as activity of the ego or voluntary
calculation of the subject.

> No more ecstasy; the feeling that he was only living because,
> even in the eyes of the Russians, he belonged to a noble class.
>   This was war: life for some, for others, the cruelty of
> assassination.

Execution here is a matter of assassination. Would one
be going too far if one were to understand this suggestion
as contesting the distinction between war and assassination, the distinctions between the right of war, the law of

peoples, the rules of war, war crime, and then murder pure
and simple? The distinction between military and civilian
loses its pertinence. The Resistance and the wars of Resistance—as Schmitt says in his *Theorie des Partisanen*—chal-
lenge the very concept of war in European law, abolishing
the distinction between military and civilian, violating the
laws of war and the law of peoples. I am jumping here to
another big chapter (Hegel, Marx, Schmitt, and Blanchot).

> There remained [*Demeurait*], however, at the moment when
> the shooting was no longer but to come, the feeling of light-
> ness that I would not know how to translate. . . .

Demeurait at the beginning: through all the mutations,
the changes of world, the conversions that have abounded
since we began, the memory *already remained* [demeurait
déjà]: the insistence and persistence of the instant, abidingly [*à demeure*] it waited and delayed, the memory of
this lightness, from the moment of lightness, from the
feeling of lightness; it already remained as it remains today still. Remaining [*Demeurer*], it was already doing this
through the entire transformation, which he is in the
process of describing in himself or in any case in the
young man. There is a memory of ecstasy, or rather the
memory of lightness, the memory of beatitude, the memory of sovereignty, which was due to the imminence of
death, to the imminence without imminence, to the imminence of a death that has already arrived. It *remained*
[demeurait], in the imperfect past of incompletion, this
lightness that has never left him, and it is difficult for him
to translate this feeling otherwise than with questions:
"freed from life?"

~

He lives, but he is no longer living. Because he is already dead, it is a life without life. All of the phrases that

Blanchot tirelessly forms according the model "X without X" ("to live without living [*vivre sans vivant*]," "to die without death [*mourir sans mort*]," "death without death," "name without name," "unhappiness without unhappiness," "being without being," etc.)[18] have their possibility, which is not only a formal possibility but an event of possibilization in what happened there, that day, at that actual instant, that is, that henceforth, starting from that stigmatic point, from the *stigma* of a verdict that condemned him to death without death being what ensued, there will be for him, for the young man, for his witness and for the author, a death without death and thus a life without life. Life has freed itself from life; one might just as well say that life has been relieved of life. A life that simply stops is neither weighty nor light. Nor is it a life that simply continues. Life can only be light from the moment that it stays dead-living while being freed, that is to say, released from itself. A life without life, an experience of lightness, an instance of "without," a logic without logic of the "X without X," or of the "not" or of the "except," of the "being without being," etc. In "A Primitive Scene," we could read: "To live without living, like dying without death: writing returns us to these enigmatic propositions."

The proof that we have here, with this testimony and reference to an event, the logical and textual matrix of Blanchot's entire corpus, so to speak, is that this lightness of "without," the thinking of the "X without X" comes to sign, consign or countersign the experience of the neuter as *ne uter, neither-nor* by bringing it together. This experience draws to itself and endures, in its very passion, the thinking as well as the writing of Blanchot, between literature and the right to death. *Neither . . . nor*: in this way the witness translates the untranslatable *demourance*:

There remained, however, at the moment when the shooting was no longer but to come, the feeling of lightness that I would not know how to translate: freed from life? the infinite opening up?

These two questions might lead one to think that the translations are inadequate. This lightness neither frees nor relieves of anything; it is neither a salvation through freedom nor an opening to the infinite because this passion is without freedom and this death without death is a confirmation of finitude. Yet here is a more affirmative response, if not a more positive and more assured one. But it is still a response according to the grammar of the *neither . . . nor*:

> Neither happiness, nor unhappiness. Nor the absence of fear and perhaps [again the perhaps] already the step beyond.

We could appeal to all of Blanchot's texts on the neuter here—the *neither-nor* that is beyond all dialectic, of course, but also beyond the negative grammar that the word neuter, *ne uter*, seems to indicate. The neuter is the experience or passion of a thinking that cannot stop at either opposite without also overcoming the opposition— neither this nor that, neither happiness nor unhappiness. The word "happiness" occurs for the second time here. He had spoken of being happy earlier: "beatitude (nothing happy, however)." "Nor the absence of fear and perhaps already the step beyond." No italics, no quotation marks, no allusion to a literary title in these words. But the logic of the book called *The Step Not Beyond* is here in some sense potentialized in this instant of death without death that signals to, without signaling, the literature of Blanchot. What is difficult to think, to analyze, to dialectize in the logic of the step beyond is not—not only—the philosophical or speculative logic that is deployed without there being anything that arrives, without there being anything that has arrived. On the contrary, it is the event, thus a passion—for the experience of what arrives must be passion, exposure to what one does not see coming and could not predict, master, calculate or program. It is *this* passion, as it is described in the instant of my death that upholds philosophy and makes possible speculative logic.

This does not mean that whoever has not almost been shot to death by the Germans cannot write, understand, or think the step beyond. What this means, and I return to the instance, to the exemplarity of the "instance," is that the logic of the step beyond assumes a singular instant of my death *in general. Singular in general.* If this text is readable, at least hypothetically, and problematically to the extent that it would be readable through and through, it would be so insofar as it is exemplary. It *refers,* it has a unique, factual, and undeniable referent—and an irreplaceable signature.

Perhaps we should insist on this difficult and no doubt decisive point, in this place of the passive and passionate decision. For in the hypothetical case of a false testimony, even one that was false through and through, and still in the hypothetical case of a lie or a phantasmatic hallucination, or indeed a literary fiction pure and simple—well then, the event described, the event of reference, will have taken place, even in its structure of "unexperienced" experience, as death without death, which one could neither say nor understand otherwise, that is, through a phantasmaticity, according to a spectrality (*phantasma* is specter in Greek) that is its very law. This spectral law both constitutes and structures the abiding [*demeurant*] reference in this narrative; it exceeds the opposition between real and unreal, actual and virtual, factual and fictional. The

death and the *demourance* of which the narrative speaks
have taken place even if they did not take place in what is
commonly called reality. The "without" in the "X without
X" signifies this spectral necessity, which overflows the opposition between reality and fiction. This spectral necessity—under certain conditions, the conditions of the
phantasma—allows what does not arrive to arrive, what
one believes does not arrive to succeed in arriving [*arriver
à arriver*]. Virtually, with a virtuality that can no longer be
opposed to actual factuality. It is here that false testimony
and literary fiction can in truth still testify, at least as
symptom, from the moment that the possibility of fiction
has structured—but with a fracture—what is called real
experience. This constituting structure is a destructuring
fracture. It is the condition that is common to literature
and non-literature, to the passion of literature as well as to
this passion *tout court* to which a literature cannot not refer. Here, in any case, the border between literature and its
other becomes undecidable. The literary institution has
imposed itself; it has also imposed the rigor of its right to
calculate, master, neutralize this undecidability, to make
as if—another fiction—literature, in its possibility, had
not begun before literature, in the very abidance [*demeurance*] of life. But it nonetheless remains [*demeure*]; one
must be able to say this just as firmly, that this undecidability, like the abyssal co-implications it engenders, does
not in the least invalidate the exigency of truthfulness,
sincerity, or objectivity, any more than it authorizes a confusion between good faith and false testimony. But the
chaos remains [*demeure*], from which alone a right [*juste*]
reference to truth emerges or arises.

It is on this condition that we understand something of
this narrative, to the extent that we understand anything at
all about it. This narrative testifies to what happened only

once, dated, occurred, arrived, even if it did not arrive, at
a date and in a place that are irreplaceable, to someone
who is, in short, the only one able to testify to it, even if he
inscribes his attestation in a network of facts largely if not
totally probable, public, accessible to proof. But this attestation both secret and public, fictional and real, literary
and non-literary—we only judge it to be readable, if it is,
insofar as a reader can understand it, even if no such thing
has ever "really" happened to *him*, to the reader. We can
speak, we can read this because this experience, in the singularity of its secret, as "experience of the unexperienced,"
beyond the distinction between the real and the phantasmatic, remains [*demeure*] universal and exemplary. We,
those to whom, I am assuming, this very thing it would
seem has never happened, and who speak French, we understand the meaning of this text up to a certain point. We
know perfectly well, however, that because this never happened to us in this way, although we understand French,
there is more than one thing that we do not understand,
that we understand without understanding. Conversely,
this thing here, this sequence of events—having almost
been shot to death, having escaped it, etc.—it is not
enough for this to have happened for the one to whom it
almost happened to understand, to be able to read this
text, and to understand and think it in the absolute secret
of its singularity. Dostoyevsky would have described the
same survival, and he would have done it altogether otherwise. He would have written, he will have written another,
very different text. Dostoyevsky is another story entirely.
What we have here is an example of this limit that trem-
bles between understanding / not understanding, speaking
French / not speaking French, speaking / not speaking.
One understands, everyone here understands this narrative
in his own way, there are as many readings as there are

readers, and yet there remains a certain manner of being in agreement with the text, if one speaks its language, provided certain conditions are met. This is testimonial exemplarity. This text bears witness to a universalizable singularity. Because this singularity is universalizable, it is able to give rise—for example, in Blanchot—to a work that depends without depending on this very event, a readable and translatable work, a work that is more and more widely translated into all the languages of the world, more or less well, etc., more or less well read in France, which does not mean that Blanchot is read better in French than he is in English.

"Neither the absence of fear and perhaps already . . . ": *perhaps*—let us count the "perhaps's" in this little book. " . . . and perhaps already the step beyond. I know . . . "—correction: "I imagine." Earlier he said: "I know—do I know." Every time he says "I know," he moderates or disturbs the knowledge: "I know—do I know. . . . "

> I know, I imagine that this unanalyzable feeling changed what there remained for him of existence.

"What there remained for him of existence" is here described as a sort of tomorrow, a sort of postscript—fifty years—this remainder that remains [*demeure*], the *demourance* of this remainder will have been but a short sequel of sorts, a fallout, a consequence. Nothing has truly begun, moreover [*au demeurant*] for fifty years, after this experience.

> As if the death outside of him could only henceforth collide with the death in him.

"As if the death outside of him": the death that came at him [*venait sur lui*] waits for Blanchot, who is still living in the same *demourance*. This death that will happen to

him could only encounter a death—so much more an-
cient—already at work in him, from the instant it has *already* happened to him. As if one only had to wait now for
the encounter, in him, like him, of these two deaths. Let
us recall what the narrator said earlier about this encounter, before a question mark: "The encounter of death
with death?" He does not know whether death is encoun-
tering death at this moment. What he knows, what he
imagines, is that, henceforth, he is still waiting for this encounter, it remains in abeyance [*demeure en instance*]. As
for him, he remains in this encounter in the moratorium
of an encounter of the death outside of him with the death
that is already dying in him. There are two deaths, and the
two die as much as they make or let die. Just as there are
two subjects—two "I's," an "I" that speaks of a young
man, an "I" that is divided by what happened there—so
there are two, concurrent deaths. One ahead of the other,
in countertime, one making an advance to the other, an
advance that it demands be returned by returning itself
[*qu'elle met en demeure de rendre en se rendant*]. They run
toward one another, into one another, one running to encounter the other. And what he knows, what he imagines
is that one death runs *after* the other: runs down, pursues
and chases, hunts the other. From the moment it chases
the other, pursues the other in order to catch up with it,
one can hypothesize that it pushes away and excludes the
death that it chases in this way, that it also protects itself in
the passion of this *permanent différance* [différance à de-
meure], of this *undying as différance* [demourance comme
différance]. What remains for him of existence, more than
this race to death, is this race of death in view of death *in
order* not to see death coming.

In order not to see it coming means three things in one:
so as not to see it coming, because one allows it to come,

and because one does not see it coming, which is death it-self. To see something coming is to anticipate, to foresee, *and* to allow to come without waiting, without preparing oneself, without seeing and knowing what comes.

Two deaths, one outside, the other inside. Which call each other back to one another.

"I am alive. No, you are dead."

The "I am alive" could be understood as the triumph of life. A fanatical jubilation. That he should have escaped death, whether or not he should have succeeded in the work of infinite mourning that should follow his own death, the survivor would be crying out in this triumphal sentence of libidinal exultation "I am alive," in the un-conscious of the "unanalyzable feeling." Like the spirit that always says *no*, the other immediately recalls him, without delay, quick as a flash, to the reality of the murder that will have taken place and cruelly repeats the verdict: "No, you are dead." We have already heard this "you are dead" in other texts by Blanchot.

But who is speaking here? Who dares proclaim, "I am alive"? Who dares reply "No, you are dead"? Up until this point, as we noted, an "I" speaks of another, of a third: "I" speaks of him. "I" is me, speaks of the young man he was, and this is still me. This is called a narration. But for the first time, between the two instances of the narrator and character, who are the same without being the same, there are quotation marks, there is speech that is being directly quoted. Someone is speaking to someone, a witness is speaking to the other for the first time, in a dialogue that is both an inner dialogue and, if I can put it this way, transcendent. "I" becomes "you" or addresses itself to "you," but we do not know whether the "I" is the one who says "I" at the beginning of the text: "I REMEMBER," or if it

is the other, the young man. We do not know *who* "you"
is, *who* says "you," nor do we know what is left out [*ce qui
est tu*] of these two instances. Like each of these sentences,
this conclusion is singularly, that is to say, properly genial.
One of the two, One of the Two, says to the Other, "I am
alive," and would thus be the one who has survived. But
it is the other, the one who has survived, who responds to
him: "No, you are dead." And this is the colloquium, this
is the dialogue between the two witnesses, who are, moreover [*au demeurant*], the same, alive and dead, living-dead,
and both of whom in abidance [*en demourance*] claim or
allege that one is alive, the other dead, as if life went only
to an *I* and death to a *you*. Always according to the same
compassion of passion.

There is a postscript. A sort of parergonal hors-d'œuvre.
After the word "death," after the death sentence of "you
are dead," one turns the page. As if there were a blank—
thus an infinite time immediately prior to the epilogue.

"Later": this is the first word of the epilogue. "Later"
not only recalls the abidance [*demourance*] and the abode
[*demeure*] of the moratorium. One would have to reread
other of Blanchot's remarkable "later's." I will cite only
one, which opens one of the two versions of "A Primitive
Scene?,"[19] a title bearing a question mark in *The Writing
of the Disaster*. And perhaps *The Instant of My Death* recounts another primitive scene with a question mark. The
first words of "A Primitive Scene?" conjugate, so to speak,
the *later* in the present indicative, addressing themselves
to the future, later, of those—the readers, the addressees—who will then live or believe they live and remember
in the present. A logic, an insane chrono-logic confides
this grammar to the law of a disjointed present, to the law
of an unlocatable present of the indicative, an anachronistic simultaneity, if you will, between the present of the

one who speaks and says "later" and the present of those who, one day, later, will read it, who are already reading it, who are put on notice [*mis en demeure*] or under house arrest [*assignés à demeure*] in this moratorium of writing. Thus: "You who live later, close to a heart that no longer beats, suppose, supposing this: the child—is he seven, perhaps eight years old? . . . " As in *The Instant of My Death*, this "primitive scene" will have begun with an allusion to the youth of the other who is none other than the ghost of the signatory, here the child, there the young man. Perhaps the child: "*perhaps* eight years old . . ."

⁓

In *The Instant of My Death*, the "later" seems simpler, one more normally attached to the *passé simple*. Is this so certain?

Later, having returned to Paris, he met [*rencontra*] Malraux.

A return to literature and a return to the world, to the literary world, this time to the world of small literary passions. A witness has just told us a story that took place during the war, on July 20, 1944, fifty-one years and four days ago. We are later. The epilogue already refers to an anterior *later*, a *later* immediately following the war: "Later, having returned to Paris . . ." (Was he thus not in Paris during the war?) Behind this first epilogal sentence an entire film passes by: the end of the war, liberation, the purges, etc. Gallimard, NRF, Paulhan, Drieu La Rochelle, etc. The whole entanglement of a very questionable history—about which we have more knowledge, but a knowledge that is also waiting for an acknowledgment, for which we have been kept waiting longer, later, than the official avowal, last week, of the responsibility of the French State in the aforementioned history, that is to say, in what since Nuremberg are called crimes against humanity. "Later, having returned to Paris, he encountered Malraux." Malraux, another "hero-of-the-Resistance" who came to the Resistance later, rather late: he, too, as did many, as did Sartre, as did so many "heroes-of-the-Resistance"—later, very late. There was a great moratorium of the Resistance for many writers during a very productive period of French literature. Later, finally, almost all of them meet up again at Gallimard, Blanchot and Malraux in any event: we can assume this given the reference to Paulhan, the *éminence grise* of the rue Sébastien-Bottin, whose figure, destiny, role, thinking, and writing during and after the war, earlier and later, bring together a good deal of the political tangle under discussion:

> Later, having returned to Paris, he met Malraux, who told him that he had been taken prisoner (without being recognized) and that he had succeeded in escaping, losing a manuscript in the process.

When two great French writers survive the war and the Occupation and meet up at Gallimard, what do they say to each other? What kind of news do they exchange? "What did you write during the war? And your manuscript?" For Malraux too lost a manuscript. Like "Blanchot," whose manuscript, we will remember or assume, was seized by the Nazi lieutenant.

> "It was only reflections on art, easy to reconstitute, whereas a manuscript would not be."

Subtle and interesting distinction—as if reflections on art were not a manuscript. Could never be confused with the writing of a manuscript. No indeed, Malraux seems to be saying, unless it is the author-narrator. The quotation marks do not make it clear, but this reflection, obligatory courtesy, would be more decent coming from one who has lost a book on art than from someone who has lost a "manuscript."

This assumes another difference. What is a manuscript if it cannot be reconstituted? It is a mortal text, a text insofar as it is exposed to a death without *survivance*. One can rewrite non-manuscripts, one can rewrite Malraux's books, they are but reflections on art whose content is not bound to the unique event and the trace of writing. It is not very serious; one can even say that these things are immortal, like a certain type of truth. But a manuscript— and this would be its definition, a definition via the end— is something whose end cannot be repeated and to which one can only testify where the testimony only testifies to the absence of attestation, namely, where nothing can testify any longer, with supporting evidence, to what has been. Pure testimony as impossible testimony. Unlike the witness-narrator, the manuscript has disappeared without remainder; it does not even have speech to recall an instant of death; it can no longer say "my death." This is what is suggested by the last sentence of this episode of literary life and the "What does it matter" that opens the final paragraph. These are perhaps—in the somewhat futile guise of an episode from literary quarters—the most simply tragic words of the narrative:

> With Paulhan, he made inquiries which could only remain in vain.

Unlike everything we have been discussing, the manuscript seems to have been lost without remainder. Nothing of it remains [*demeure*]. Unless one could say: without remainder other than *The Instant of My Death*, than the narrative entitled *The Instant of My Death*, its last witness, a supplementary substitute which, by recalling its disappearance, replaces it without replacing it. The absolute loss, perdition without salvation and without repetition, would have been that of a piece of writing. To which one can but testify, beyond all present attestation, however.

Let us listen now to what will be said in order to end "more precisely." Let us listen "more precisely":

> What does it matter. All that remains is the feeling of lightness that is death itself or, to put it more precisely, the instant of my death henceforth always in abeyance.

This final, added precision, this precision more, this "more precisely" bears the final signature of this remarkable narrative. It must therefore not remain inaudible or weakly perceptible. The "more precisely" admits that it is not a question of "death itself," that it has never been a question of testifying to "death itself." This little word "itself [*même*]" is crossed out by the compunction of the witness, as if he were saying: What remains in the abidance [*demourance*], that of which the feeling of lightness[20] is a symptom or a truth, is not death *itself*, the being or the essence or what belongs to death, to the event *itself*, the *itself* or the *Selbst* of death properly speaking. There is not death properly speaking. It is not "death itself"; death itself is properly prohibited.

Permanently even [*A demeure même*].

What there is is only, "more precisely," the instance of the instant of my death, the instance of my death always in abeyance—in every sense, according to all the instances of the word *instance* that we have seen condensed, displaced, suspended, that we have seen as they themselves remain in abeyance, waiting to be handed over, delivered, judged. According to a term about which it is difficult to say that it remains to come.

The association of "always" with "henceforth" ("hence-

forth always in abeyance [*désormais toujours en instance*]")
countersigns the abidance [*la demourance*]. The persistence of *always*, as instance of the *aiōn*, this Greek word
meaning time, the duration of a life, a generation, all of
life, both the present time and endless eternity, is here
combined with "henceforth," which signifies "from now
on and in the future," thus "later": always later, the future
always later, the permanent future [*l'avenir à demeure*].
Permanently even [*A demeure même*]. With the word *doré-
navant*, which means almost the same thing as *désormais*,
without having exactly the same grammatical relation to
time, the adverb *désormais* is for me one of the most beautiful, and one of the most untranslatable, words, in a
word, in the French language.

In order to ask your pardon for having made things go
on so long, in order to end without ending in great haste,
and since I have only spoken, in French, of the French
language and French literature, here are several *désormais*'s
with which both the French language and French literature have distinguished themselves.

These *désormais*'s all say—and it is certainly not in-
significant—something about the compassion and the
"complaining" to which, as with remainders, as with a
talk, one must know how to put an end.

Corneille, first, in *Cinna*: "On portera le joug *désormais*
sans se plaindre [We will bear the yoke *henceforth* without
complaining]."

La Fontaine, next, whose memory is being celebrated
these days:

> *Désormais* que ma muse, aussi bien que mes jours,
> Touche de son déclin l'inévitable cours,
> Et que de ma raison le flambeau va s'éteindre,
> Irai-je en consumer les restes à me plaindre?

Henceforth given that my muse, as well as my days,
Draw to their inevitable close,
And that the flame of my reason will soon be
    extinguished,
Shall I consume what remains of them by
    complaining?

(*Poésies mêlées*)

Amyot finally, the French patron of translation, the translator of *Parallel Lives* and the *Lives* of Plutarch. He knew to write this: "C'est *désormais* assez discouru sur ce point [*Henceforth*, enough has been said on this point]."

Reading "beyond the beginning"; or, On the Venom in Letters

Postscript and "Literary Supplement"

Curtius, thus. A brief allusion to Curtius, too brief, of course, gives me the opportunity to take up an insult. Serious, comic, and symptomatic at once. A venomous "Letter to the Editor" (J. Drake, *Times Literary Supplement* [*TLS*], May 2, 1997) has just been published, which takes as its pretext another allusion to Curtius, even more brief, that I made more than thirty years ago in *De la grammatologie* (Minuit, 1967, p. 27). I devoted several lines then to "The symbolism of the book, this beautiful chapter in *European Literature and the Latin Middle Ages*."

Should one respond to a correspondent who first confuses several of Plato's dialogues with each other and then the discussion with the injury? When one is not oneself discouraged by such attacks, should they be encouraged by being taken seriously?

Should one respond, taking the risk of legitimating methods so harmful to discussion, to research, and, finally, to the public and academic space?

Should one respond to hate-filled gesticulations when they proceed with such worrisome signs of ignorance or obscurantism?

Should one respond *in* a journal that seems to make
these rantings against me a sort of specialty, a genre in itself—from the time, I am told, I was awarded an honorary
doctorate by Cambridge University? This great and presti-
gious university would thus have committed, by usurpa-
tion as it were, a no doubt unforgivable mistake in the eyes
of certain distinguished intellectuals, English or not, the
very ones who are made fun of—another inadmissible out-
rage—by a recent book (*Derrida for Beginners*), one of
those comic-strip volumes that the venerable *TLS* has
never reviewed, except, that is, on this occasion, as if to
launch the offensive I am talking about (cf. R. Harris,
"Fiddle, fiddle, fiddle," *TLS*, March 21, 1997). Mr. Harris's
article begins, furthermore, with a protest in nationalistic
style on the subject of this honorary doctorate. Attacking
thus, he concludes with a strange word of advice ("above all
do not read!") given to the "beginners" (in the name of the
Lumières or the Enlightenment, I suppose): they are not to
be tempted to venture beyond the beginning in their reading, in the reading of a book that concerns me, of course. I
quote: "*The worst fate in store for beginners here would be
that they might be tempted to venture beyond the beginning.*"
I suppose it is this excellent advice, this enlightened rec-
ommendation for reading that seduced a French journal
from Montpelier, which I discovered on this occasion; it
translates this luminous article under a magnificent title, in
which friends will recognize me: "The Nero of Philosophy." (That's me. Ah, the Enlightenment! Always more
light! As for the title of the journal that thus advises one
not to read, it is equally flamboyant: *The Reader!*)

To return to *TLS*: this last injurious letter, that of Mr.
Drake, belongs thus to a series of analogous and equally
furious missives. They cite one another. They pass each
other the torch and they all return, one after the other, to

the code and to the words of those who, at Cambridge and elsewhere, loudly declared war on the occasion of this doctorate: on my work, on my person, and on those who refer to them.

Should one respond, finally, above all, in a journal that does not respect the most elementary standard of professional ethics, a standard that would consist in asking in advance the person under attack or slandered if he or she wishes to respond in the *same* issue? (For I admit I am not a regular reader, to say the least, of this strange journal that *TLS* is or is becoming. When I do not happen upon these attacks in an airport, I am only informed of them long after, indirectly, thanks to worried or indignant friends.) What is more, to respond *in a journal*, even after the fact, to a series of abuses published by the *same journal*, one must, as far as the handling of the response is concerned, have confidence, something, alas, I have on more than one occasion learned to lose.

This is why, henceforth, I take my precautions: when at least I believe I must respond, I do so without haste, on a date, in a form, and in a situation that are appropriate to the seriousness of what I want to say.

Here the following, very simply: after an attentive re-reading of all the texts evoked and incriminated, I have found nothing to change in what I wrote (which was, moreover, very laudatory) about Curtius in 1967. I would give the exact same response to earlier attacks in the same style, in the same journal (B. Vickers, "Letters to the Editor," May 9, 1997) on the subject of what I wrote (which was, moreover, very laudatory) about Peirce and Saussure in *De la grammatologie* (p. 7ff for the former; Part I, chapter 2, for the latter). If I have understood the attacks (I am not certain about this, since, so far as clarity and the ability to demonstrate are concerned, the argumentation of the lesson-givers is not a model of the genre), and if I put them face to face with the texts incriminated, I still see no infamy to expose, no lapse to detect or to regret in the logic of what I wrote thirty years ago and about which my censors seem to know nothing. This may seem presumptuous, but I will not pretend to own up to mistakes out of politeness, in order to appear modest or simply to make the signatories of letters that are so spiteful feel good. I really think—if they want to understand—that they must "venture beyond the beginning."

I can only insist here, in conclusion, on this point, one that is, in my eyes, vital to the pursuit of this debate: by giving, as I have just done, all of the necessary references (something which the scholarly correspondents of *TLS* do not do), I mean to help the interested reader and invite this reader to come to his or her own opinion, that is, to reread and patiently analyze *all* of the documents in this case. But for this, yes, the reader will indeed have to "venture beyond the beginning."

In order to reconstitute a context and arrive at some idea of the way in which my censors have engaged the polemic and launched the assault, I would advise beginning, of course, with the letter of someone who, quoting the previous issues of *TLS*, suspects me of "intellectual charlatanism" at the very same moment that, on two separate occasions—which cannot be accidental—he confuses *Phaedrus* with *Phaedo*. Nothing less. Is this not worrisome on the part of a guardian who is so jealously preoccupied with reserving for himself the right to interpret a philologist and historian of great repute? What would the great Curtius have thought of a "scholar" who, coming to his rescue, does not see the difference between two of Plato's dialogues, just because the two titles both begin with *Ph*? *Ph*, as in *pharmakon*, this poison-remedy to which letters are compared: and this in *Phaedrus,* not *Phaedo.* If Mr. Drake would like to read Plato one day, he would see a difference, this difference at least to begin with.

And later—I hope for him and his allies in this campaign—perhaps he will also discern the dangers of confusion. When one begins to read one should not, above all, follow the advice of the author of "The Nero of Philosophy." In order to escape obscurantism, one must, on the contrary, I repeat my advice, always, always *"venture beyond the beginning."*

Notes

Notes

1. The only title I submitted before the conference was "Fiction and Testimony."

2. Cf. Jacques Derrida, *Mémoires—pour Paul de Man* (Paris: Galilée, 1988), p. 44; Jacques Derrida, *Memoires for Paul de Man*, trans. Cecile Lindsay, Jonathan Culler, Eduardo Cadava, and Peggy Kamuf (New York: Columbia University Press, 1989), p. 22.

3. Cited in A. Berman, *L'épreuvre de l'étranger*, (Paris: Gallimard, 1984), pp. 95–96.

4. Cited in ibid., p. 91.

5. E. R. Curtius, *European Literature and the Latin Middle Ages*, trans. Willard Trask (Princeton: Princeton University Press, 1953), p. 16.

6. Ibid., p. 12.

7. Ibid., p. 13. Concerning Curtius, see the Postscript, "Reading 'beyond the beginning.'"

8. "Foi et savoir: Les deux sources de la religion aux limites de la raison," in Jacques Derrida and Gianni Vattimo, eds., *Religion: Séminaire de Capri* (Paris: Seuil, 1995); "Faith and Knowledge: The Two Sources of 'Religion' at the Limit of Reason Alone," trans. Samuel Weber, in Jacques Derrida and Gianni Vattimo, eds., *Religion* (Stanford: Stanford University Press, 1998), pp. 1–78.

9. M. Blanchot, *Le pas au-delà* (Paris: Gallimard, 1973), p. 107; M. Blanchot, *The Step Not Beyond*, trans. Lynette Nelson (Albany: State University of New York Press, 1992), p. 76. [Throughout, I have at times silently altered published translations where need be to better reflect aspects of the original text under discussion.—Trans.]

10. M. Blanchot, *L'écriture du désastre* (Paris: Gallimard, 1980), p. 105 (my emphasis); M. Blanchot, *The Writing of the Disaster*, trans. Ann Smock (Lincoln: University of Nebraska Press, 1986), p. 64. Mallarmé also speaks of "*l'Hôte*," "regarding the book." [In following notes, the English page number of a citation follows the French page number, separated by a solidus.—Trans.]

11. Ibid., p. 110/67 (my emphasis).

12. Ibid., p. 70/41.

13. Ibid., pp. 108–9/65–66.

14. The quotations from *The Instant of My Death* will henceforth follow on from one another without the least departure from Blanchot's text—which we will attempt to follow word by word.

15. Peggy Kamuf is the author of an admirable and as yet unpublished translation of *L'instant de ma mort.*

16. In fact or in truth (but here again is something which signs the difference between fiction and testimony) the date 1807 is slightly erroneous. Jena was occupied by the French on Monday, October 13, 1806. As Michel Lisse has since reminded me, on this date Hegel writes at length to Niethammer—concerning one of these manuscript stories, about which we will speak further: "I have such worries about sending off the manuscript last Wednesday and Friday, as you can see by the date.—Last night at around sunset I saw the gunshots fired by the French. . . . I saw the Emperor—this spirit of the world—leave the city to go on reconnaissance; it is indeed a wonderful sensation to see such an individual who, concentrated in a single point, sitting on a horse, extends over the world and dominates it. . . . given what is happening, I am forced to ask myself if my manuscript, which was sent off Wednesday and Friday

has arrived; my loss would indeed be too great; the people that I know have suffered nothing; must I be the only one?"

Hegel must, like his landlord, have left his house to the French soldiers. Several days later, to the same Niethammer, he specifies: "Your house at Leitergasse (where I stayed several hours) was, it is true, in danger of fire. . . . As I have been pillaged here. . . If in the end one of the packets of the manuscript is lost, my presence will be altogether necessary; it is true that these people have put my papers in such disorder" (October 18, 1806). Several days later, to the same: "[H]ow lucky for the French and for us that we have this weather! If the wind had been blowing, the entire city would have been reduced to ashes!" (October 22, 1806).

Dichtung und Wahrheit: salvation for another castle, before other troops of occupation. Goethe to his friends in Jena on October 18 of the same year: "In my house, nothing has been damaged, I have lost nothing. . . . The castle is intact." (Cf. Hegel, *Correspondance 1. 1785–1812*, trans. J. Carrère [Paris: Gallimard, 1962], pp. 115–19).

And always in the name of the salvation of the trace, here of the manuscript to be saved, at the instant of death, during the Second World War, the following, which Michel Lisse has also brought to my attention: "Whatever happens, the manuscript must be saved. It is more important than my own person" (Walter Benjamin to Lisa Fittko, cited by Bernd Witte, *Walter Benjamin: Une biographie*, trans. André Bernold [Paris: Le Cerf, 1988], p. 253).

17. Hegel to Niethammer, on the same October 22, 1806: "In this general misery, your friendship brings me such consolation and help! Without this help, I do not know what state I would be in!" (Hegel, *Correspondance 1*, p. 118).

18. I have tried to analyze these elsewhere. Cf. *Parages* (Paris: Galilée, 1986), p. 91 and *passim*.

19. Blanchot, *L'écriture du désastre*, p. 117; Blanchot, *The Writing of the Disaster*, p. 72.

20. The instance of the instant, the instant of death promised by verdict or condemnation, an ecstatic feeling of libera-

tion and lightness, does all this not impose a movement or a moment of "grace," of "true grace" on this "passion"? Like a salvation? A forgiveness suddenly indifferent to salvation? At the instant of rereading these pages one last time, I remember a passage from *Thomas the Obscure*. I had *already* forgotten it at the moment I quoted it in *La carte postale* on August 17, 1979. Allow me to cite the citation of this forgetting: "[H]e [Pierre, my son] rarely leaves his room (guitar, records, his type-writer noisier and more regular than mine, I'm downstairs), yesterday it was to show me this passage from *Thomas the Obscure* (I'll tell you how he fell upon it) that I had totally forgotten, although two or three years ago I had commented on it at length: ' . . . I was even the only possible dead man, I was the only man who did not give the impression of dying by chance. All of my strength, the feeling that I had of being, when taking the hemlock, not Socrates dying, but Socrates augmenting himself with Plato, that certainty of not being able to disappear possessed only by those who are struck with a fatal illness, that serenity before the scaffold which gives to the condemned their true grace, made each instant of my life the instant when I was going to quit life'" (Jacques Derrida, *The Post Card: From Socrates to Freud and Beyond*, trans. Alan Bass [Chicago: University of Chicago Press, 1987], p. 243).

M E R I D I A N

Crossing Aesthetics

Massimo Cacciari, *Posthumous People: Vienna at the Turning Point*

David E. Wellbery, *The Specular Moment: Goethe's Early Lyric and the Beginnings of Romanticism*

Edmond Jabès, *The Little Book of Unsuspected Subversion*

Hans-Jost Frey, *Studies in Poetic Discourse: Mallarmé, Baudelaire, Rimbaud, Hölderlin*

Pierre Bourdieu, *The Rules of Art: Genesis and Structure of the Literary Field*

Nicolas Abraham, *Rhythms: On the Work, Translation, and Psychoanalysis*

Jacques Derrida, *On the Name*

David Wills, *Prosthesis*

Maurice Blanchot, *The Work of Fire*

Jacques Derrida, *Points . . . : Interviews, 1974–1994*

J. Hillis Miller, *Topographies*

Philippe Lacoue-Labarthe, *Musica Ficta (Figures of Wagner)*

Jacques Derrida, *Aporias*

Emmanuel Levinas, *Outside the Subject*

Jean-François Lyotard, *Lessons on the Analytic of the Sublime*

Peter Fenves, *"Chatter": Language and History in Kierkegaard*

Jean-Luc Nancy, *The Experience of Freedom*

Jean-Joseph Goux, *Oedipus, Philosopher*

Haun Saussy, *The Problem of a Chinese Aesthetic*

Jean-Luc Nancy, *The Birth to Presence*

Library of Congress Cataloging-in-Publication Data

Blanchot, Maurice.
  [Instant de ma mort. English]
  The instant of my death / Maurice Blanchot. Demeure /
Jacques Derrida ; [translated by Elizabeth Rottenberg].
    p.   cm. — (Meridian)
    Includes bibliographical references and index.
    ISBN 0-8047-3325-2 (cloth : alk. paper) — ISBN 0-8047-3326-0
(paper : alk. paper)
    I. Blanchot, Maurice—Criticism and interpretation.
I. Rottenberg, Elizabeth.   II. Derrida, Jacques. Demeure.
English.   III. Title: Demeure.   IV. Title.   V. Meridian
(Stanford, Calif.)
PC2603.L3343 I57   2000
843'.912—dc21   99-462364

Original printing 2000
Last figure below indicates the year of this printing:
09   08   07   06   05   04   03   02   01   00

Typeset by James P. Brommer
in 10.9/13 Garamond and Lithos display